Impact of Religion on Bus
in Europe and the Musl

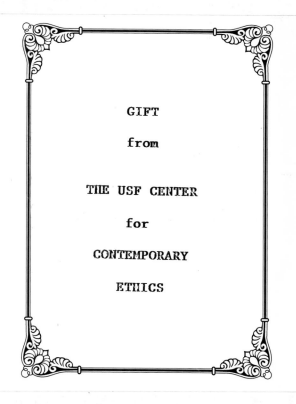

Ingmar Wienen

Impact of Religion on Business Ethics in Europe and the Muslim World

Islamic versus Christian Tradition

2nd, revised edition

PETER LANG

Frankfurt am Main · Berlin · Bern · New York · Paris · Wien

Die Deutsche Bibliothek - CIP-Einheitsaufnahme

Wienen, Ingmar:

Impact of religion on business ethics in Europe and the Muslim
world : Islamic versus Christian tradition / Ingmar Wienen. -
2nd, revised edition. - Frankfurt am Main ; Berlin ; Bern ; New
York ; Paris ; Wien : Lang, 1999
　　　ISBN 3-631-34537-2

ISBN 3-631-34537-2
US-ISBN 0-8204-4314-X

© Peter Lang GmbH
Europäischer Verlag der Wissenschaften
Frankfurt am Main 1997
2nd, revised edition 1999
All rights reserved.

Printed in Germany 1 2 3 4　6 7

To my parents

"Not all of them are alike: of the
People of the Book are a portion
that stand [for the right]; they
rehearse the signs of ALLAH all
night long, and they prostate
themselves in adoration."

(Koran 3:113)

"The God said to Abraham: 'As
for you, you must keep my
covenant, you and your
descendants after you for the
generations to come.'"

(Genesis 17:9)

Acknowledgements

This research project would not have been possible without the support of a number of people:

- my tutor, Dr. Paul Robins, who provided me with encouragement, critique and help to do an academic research project,

- my fellow students with whom I had very encouraging discussions about ethics, and especially Sandra Brugger, Heiko Lüpkes, Bruno Moncorgé, David Ryan and Axel Schmitz who gave me valuable support,

- The European Business Ethics Network which created a great environment for reflections about the subject,

- The Institute of Islamic Banking and Insurance, London, which helped me in establishing contacts in the Islamic banking community,

- The Islamic Foundation, Markfield, Leicestershire, which gave me valuable advice.

- Finally, I would like to thank the ambassadors to Germany of the following countries for their help in establishing contacts to banks in their countries: The Republic of Indonesia, The Republic of Malaysia, The Democratic Socialist Republic of Sri Lanka, India, Pakistan, The Arab Republic of Egypt, The Islamic Republic of Mauritania, The Republic of South Africa, The Republic of Turkey and Switzerland.

Preface for the second edition

It is a great pleasure to prepare a second edition of a book so shortly after the first. The whole contents have been carefully revisited and attention has been given to all suggestions made so far.

I hope that this book will continue to contribute to the discussion on the relationship between religion and business practices in different cultural settings. I would like to encourage the readers of this book to send their comments to me by e-mail: 74012.3640@compuserve.com.

Amsterdam, November 1998
Ingmar M. Wienen

List of contents

CHAPTER III.
THEORETICAL STUDY:

CHAPTER V.
EMPIRICAL STUDY:

List of tables

List of illustrations

List of abbreviations

AG	Aktiengesellschaft, "joint-stock company"
AMF	Arab Monetary Fund (established 1976)
Arab Fund	Arab Fund for Economic and Social Development (established 1971)
BCE	before common era
CE	common era, (anno domini)
cf.	confer, "compare"
d.	died
ed.	editor
eds.	editors
eG	eingetragene Genossenschaft, "registered co-operative"
esp.	especially
et al.	and others
etc.	et cetera
i.e.	id est
Iran Org.	Organization for Investment, Economic and Technical Assistance of Iran (established 1975)
IsDB	Islamic Development Bank (established 1975)
Kuwait Fund	Kuwait Fund for Arab Economic Development (established 1961)
Ltd	Limited
N/A	not applicable
OIC	Organisation of Islamic Conference
OPEC	Organization of the Petroleum Exporting Countries
OPEC Fund	OPEC Fund for International Development (established 1976)
S.A.	Société Anonyme, "joint-stock company"
Saudi Fund	The Saudi Fund for Development (established 1974)
VIF	Venezuelan Investment fund (established 1974)

CHAPTER I.

PROBLEM DEFINITION AND RESEARCH OBJECTIVES

A. Research focus

The world gets more and more **interconnected**. International trade is increasing, regional and world-wide co-operation is getting ever more close while information is available at a global level.

In consequence, decisions are increasingly taken under the influence of different environments involving more and more people from **different cultural backgrounds**. These differences need reflection so that both sides can learn from them.

It is therefore important that there are effective common or accepted standards and practices so as not to hinder interactions. The need for common ethical standards to be applied generally does not mean that everybody should adhere to the same standard and give up the initial one but that **the intersection of the different standards should be large enough**. This implies an increasing importance of cultural aspects of business decisions and the **underlying values and principles**.

One aspect of culture that may have a large effect on ethical principles and standards is the **influence of religion**. In fact, there are business modes which are linked explicitly to religion. To illustrate this, one needs only refer to medieval times, when Jews were particular familiar as moneylenders, a profession which was forbidden to Christians. This gave rise to the discreditation of Jews as extortionate people who drive hard bargains. External to the world of business, there are also examples for links between religion and organisational life. One could refer to international organisations such as the Red Cross and the Red Crescent:

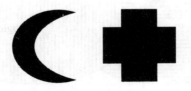

Illustration 1. Symbols of Red Cross and Red Crescent

17

Both organisations have similar objectives, but there are separate structures for Christians and Muslims.

It would appear, then, that the influence of religions may hinder rather than support the establishment of a common business ethic as they differ considerably in their doctrines and practices.

Traditionally, the reflection on the different factors guiding business activities has been the domain of economics, business ethics, theology etc. as individual disciplines. One of the problems was that reflection on business ethics as part of theology often neglected the restrictions and pressures of "real-life" business situations and remained in an ivory tower. On the other hand, reflection on business ethics within the domain of economics often lead to a pure opportunism if the impact of what could be referred to as "fundamental values" was neglected.

Throughout this theses, "business ethics" is understood as the set of standards and behaviour in business. The concern of this research project is therefore to assess the extent to which religion influences **standards and behaviour in business** from a perspective taking into account theological *and* economic aspects. It also tries to find out whether an influence is only exerted in business modes which refer explicitly to religion or in other practices as well.

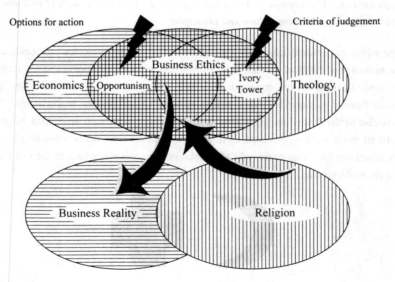

Illustration 2. Focus of this research project

B. Research objective

The objective is to develop a better understanding of cross-cultural business with a view to finding ways of improving the interaction by referring to common ethical standards.

At this point, various research designs are possible:

1. to compare one business mode in two environments of different religions: One could observe a given business mode, i.e. the sale of **environmentally friendly** body care, and look for differences within a North-American and an Asian environment,

2. to compare two business modes referring directly to two different religions in one environment: One could look at butcher's shops run by **Jews** and by **Muslims** in Europe, slaughtering according to Jewish and Muslim requirements, or

3. to compare two business modes referring directly to two different religions in two environments largely influenced by the two religions involved: One could look at butcher's shops run by Jews and by Muslims in **Tel Aviv** and in **Ankara**.

None of the above however would allow to asses whether an influence of religion on standards and behaviour in business is only exerted in business modes which refer directly to religion or in other practices as well. The reason is, that either only one business mode is researched or only modes referring directly to religion(s) are taken into consideration.

- The strategic design of the research is therefore

- to choose a business sector as a sample which both (1) operates in different cultural environments and (2) in which some modes of operation refer explicitly to religious values while others do not refer explicitly to religious values but still have an ethical claim. As an entire business sector is too broad a subject for examination in the time available the comparison will be focused mainly to one sub-sector; for the same reason the comparison will be focused on two different cultural environments only.

- The next logical step will then be to compare current practices in each of the four combinations of environment and mode of operation to identify the differences and similarities.

- Finally, explanations were sought for any differences found.

19

For this research, the **finance sector** was chosen because it is one of the few sectors which is already operating at a global level (request 1). The second reason for choosing the finance sector was that there are some banks and insurances which operate in a way referring explicitly to Islamic ethics as "Islamic banks" and "Islamic insurances", while other banks operate as "co-operative banks" which do not refer explicitly to religious values but still have an ethical claim (request 2). An "Islamic bank" is a bank claiming to obey to Islamic law, which requires amongst others that no riba or interest is paid. A "co-operative bank" on the other hand is a bank belonging to a union of people, the profits being shared among its members.

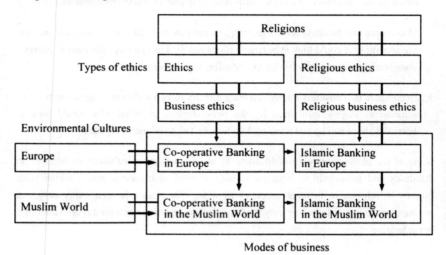

Illustration 3. Strategic research design

As far as **environments** are concerned, the Muslim World was chosen, because Islam is a driving force behind the cultural development in the Muslim World. Therefore, it is the same religion that is referred to in the business under review and that plays a dominant role in one of the environments.[1] It is important to note that the term "Muslim World" is used as a geographical term.[2] As Europe provides a good example for increasing inter-connection of countries itself but also has to define its relations with its neighbours, it was taken for a comparison with its geographical neighbour, the Muslim World. One aspect

---

[1] Other important religions like Buddhism had interaction with Muslim countries.

[2] The terms "Europe" and the "Muslim World" will be explained in detail on page 27.

of European culture is the influence that Christianity has had on it.[3] This implies that Islam as dominant **religion** in the geographical area called the Muslim World should be compared to Christianity as dominant religion in Europe.

Furthermore, little comparative research on the subject has been done so far in this sector.

C. Research questions

This research project will deal with the fact that within the Muslim World and also within Europe, there is the practice of "Islamic Banking". What exactly would be the influence of Islam on these banks?

Secondly, the influence of religion on co-operative banks will be dealt with. Would Islam have an impact on co-operative banks in the Muslim World? Is there an influence of Christian Faith on co-operative banks in Europe?

On the basis of this second research, is it be possible to describe "ethical" banking? Would this consist of one or several ethical systems?

As the objective is to develop a better understanding of cross-cultural business with a view to finding ways of improving the interaction, the overall question is: Would there be potential for co-operation between Muslims and Christians, i.e. is there any common ethical ground for these two religions?

---

[3] In Europe, Judaism has also played a very important role, partly by the role that large minorities have played and partly through the common heritage of the Judaeo-Christian bible tradition.

CHAPTER II.

STATE-OF-THE-ART REVIEW

A. Introduction

The objective of an extensive literature research was to clarify which research had pre-viously been carried out that could provide answers to the research questions.

Some of the work done in intercultural studies is presented in the following. Furthermore, a number of important researchers on religion are included in the review as well. In addition to this, several researchers having written on ethics and economics from an ethical point of view are considered, such as Adam Smith and Max Weber.

B. Intercultural studies

As far as the objective to develop a better understanding of cross-cultural business is con-cerned, **Hofstede** has published extensive research on the interdependence of culture, organisations and management. He has developed five categories that determine the differences between nations, organisations and companies:[4]

1. the degree of integration of the individual in groups,

2. the differences of social roles between men and women,

3. ways to deal with inequality,

4. tolerance of the unknown and

5. long-term versus short-term satisfaction of needs.

This has led him to giving advice on how to cope with a given culture which he sees as important within business.

---

[4] Cf. Hofstede (1993, 152-155).

Hofstede deals with religion as one determining entity within culture. He has described a significant correlation between some of his categories and religions. In several dimensions, Muslim countries seem to be quite different from countries with a Christian majority.

Trompenaars has tried to give answers on how to integrate local cultures and international environment or how to gain an international dimension in companies that do business on an international level. He is quite opposed to mainstream thinking that there are cultural stereotypes. He argues that a culture may well have dominating characteristics. However, there is a cultural identity of each individual person and company which enables it to adapt to a wide range of contexts. He suggests a set of seven cultural dimensions.[5]

In a more applied way, **Usunier** has shown the impact of culture on marketing in an international context.[6] Similar to Hofstede, Usunier describes religion as one source of culture. He shows that as a consequence of dealing with different cultures, products may have to be adapted, negotiations reviewed or partners to be searched.

Hermel has studied extensively the reality of management on a European and international level with a special emphasises on the aspect of human resource management. His results have the merit to show that within Europe there are large differences.[7]

A major overview of comparative research on management cultures in the German speaking world has been published by **Keller**. He defines culture as all shared implicit and explicit rules for behaviour that are passed from one generation to the next. In his research he points to the weaknesses of quantitative intercultural research and favours a qualitative approach.[8]

Dülfer has published a major work that demonstrates the potential long-term applications of international management. He argues that companies will become increasingly global and therefore have to understand international business customs. Like Hofstede, Dülfer looks at the influence of religion on international management as one of several ethical

---

[5] Trompenaars (1994).

[6] Usunier (1992a, 61-66).

[7] Hermel (1993).

[8] Von Keller (1982).

standards influenced by culture. He has provided valuable material on the impact of Islam on business. However, he has not sufficiently analysed the European position which would have enabled him to really compare the two systems.[9]

To sum up, it is recognised by several researchers that international business is influenced by the interaction of different cultures which in turn are influenced by religion. However, a more direct link between religion and business has not been established yet.

C. Studies on religions

There are eight religions in the world which combine beliefs and the introduction of ethical standards:

1. Brahmanism or Hinduism,
2. Jainism,
3. Buddhism,
4. Chinese Universalism,
5. Zoroastrianism or Parsism,
6. Judaism,
7. Christianity and
8. Islam.

Out of those, Hinduism, Buddhism, Chinese Universalism, Christianity and Islam are the most important by numbers. Together, they represent 90 % of the "religious world".

Von Glasenapp has published one of the major guides to the world religions. He separates the five religions named above into two groups: Eastern and Western religions. He characterises Eastern religions as religions of an "eternal law", whereas western religions argue that the existence of the world and its inhabitants depends on a powerful God who created all out of nothing by his own power. While eastern religions do not think that the world has a beginning and an end, western religions teach that it has started at some point and that it will end at some time.[10]

Christianity and Islam are, according to this definition, Western religions as opposed to Hinduism or Buddhism. This classification may appear astonishing to Europeans who

---

[9] Dülfer (1992, 281-290).

[10] Von Glasenapp (1994, 9-12).

think that Islam comes from the South and East. However it underlines how close Christianity and Islam are compared to other world religions.

Both religions have a tendency to be exclusive and also all-encompassing. As a consequence, history provides numerous instances of conflicts during the encounters of Christianity and Islam.

Le Gai Eaton has described that the Christian faith spread out virtually without limitation after its acceptance as the state religion of the late Roman empire. The starting point of the relation between Christianity and Islam is the fact that Christianity only experienced resistance when Islam came into being.[11] Islam now broadened its base with great success and was only stopped in 732 in Tours and Poitiers by Charles Martel. From the XIth to the XIIIth century, the crusades were organised against Islam.

Europeans have imagined Mohammed, the prophet of Islam, as a cruel politician or even as incarnation of the evil: Pope Innocent III, 1160-1216, identified him as the Anti-Christ and took the initiative for the fourth crusade. In the centuries that followed, Islam would come back with the Turkish armies that twice arrived in Vienna.

In summary, Christianity and Islam should be seen as two religions with intensive theological and historical links.

D. Studies on ethics and on business ethics

Before one can go more into the details about business ethics, several important differentiations about the term "ethics" itself have to be made.

Arthur Rich has shown that ethics can be *analytical* and reflect on fundamental words as "good" or "justice", purely *descriptive* and record what happens, or it can be *normative* and define how or even what decisions should be taken.

Within *normative* ethics Rich differentiates

- an "ethic of convictions" or "rule-based ethics": a number of fundamental rules are defined. Any decisions have to be made according to those rules: if the decision is coherent with the rule, it will be accepted as good, otherwise it must be rejected.

---

[11] Cf. Le Gai Eaton (1994, 24-27).

- an ethic of "responsibility" or "outcome-focused ethics": a number of "good" goals, that are to be achieved, are formulated. Decisions are accepted as good if they lead to the fulfilment of the goal, otherwise they are rejected.

One could say that while an ethic of convictions does care less about the outcome as long as the "good" means are used, an ethic of responsibility cares less about the means, by which a "good" goal is achieved.[12]

Bruno Staffelbach distinguishes *normative* ethics even further: those approaches treating the basis of ethical norms as a cognitivistic problem are summarised as *monologistic* approaches. Approaches basing ethical norms on social interaction are grouped as *dialogistic* approaches.[13] Within *monologistic* approaches, Staffelbach presents similarly to Rich's "rule-based ethics" and "outcome-focused ethics"

- "deontological approaches", in which maxims count (δεον, Greek: duty). The perfect example of that kind of ethic is **Immanuel Kant** (1724-1804), who formulated the *Categorical Imperative*: "You should only act according to the maxim which you would want to be general law."[14] **Gandz** and **Hayes** have called political and religious fundamentalism a new form of deontological ethics: "Whose adherents believe that there is a single, universal moral standard and that they know what is right".[15]

Another direction within this group are theories of fairness: they reckon that there is not only one single duty, but possibly several duties. **John Rawls** has suggested two basic principles: "First: each person is to have an equal right to the most extensive basic liberty compatible with a similar liberty for others. Second: social and economic inequalities are to be arranged so that they are both (a) reasonably expected to be to everyone's advantage, and (b) attached to positions and offices open to all."[16]

- "teleological approaches", in which results count. This can be egoistic - based on self-interest - or utilitaristic - based on general interest or general welfare.

---

[12] Rich (1984, 20-40) provides a good introduction into these differences.

[13] Staffelbach (1994, 149-167).

[14] Kant (1968).

[15] Gandz / Hayes (1988).

[16] Rawls (1972).

As *dialogistic* approach is followed by **Peter Ulrich**. He defines an interactive-communicative approach as constitutive anthropological.[17]

The classical moral philosopher and economist **Adam Smith** (1723-1790) defined "general welfare" as an objective in the economic process. He formulated fundamental ethical assumptions about motivations and markets in his work "An inquiry into the nature and causes of the wealth of Nations".[18] One of them, the self-interest, has been widely over-emphasised. Therefore, a great part of today's economic theory is based on the idea of self-interest maximisation, which is a very narrow estimation of human behaviour.

Max Weber has shown on the turn of the 19th to the 20th century that economy can indeed only be explained if ethical elements are taken into consideration. He demonstrated the influence of the Protestant tradition on German business and social behaviour. At the same time, he asserted that Islam was at its best in medieval times but then entered into decline which included economic decline.[19]

Following to Weber's research, the question was raised whether the Islamic concept of labour and production contributed to this decline of Islam in that trust in God or *tawakkul* would lead to passivity in economic affairs.[20] Islamic thinkers pointed out however, that Islam is in favour of development and can therefore not be responsible for all economic troubles.[21]

This could not prevent the divorce of modern economics and ethics. Only recently it has been recognised that economics cannot be understood without ethics.[22] More particularly, business can no longer be understood without taking into account religious traditions.

Wilson, one of the leading European experts on Islamic economics, points out two ethical principles in the Islamic business world which are based on religious traditions: the ban of

---

[17] Ulrich (1990, 1993), Ulrich / Fluri (1992).

[18] Smith (1981).

[19] Weber (1993).

[20] Please refer to page 131 for an overview of Arabic terms.

[21] Cf. Klöcker, Tworuschka and Tworuschka (1995, 22).

[22] Cf. Sen (1987).

riba and the commandment of *zakat*.[23] Both are linked to the Islamic concept of justice: Everybody has to earn his own income, but he also has to assist those in difficulties. The terms *zakat* and *riba* being key terms will be explained in detail on pages 40 and 43.[24]

One important attempt to formulate the moral foundations of international business is the so-called stakeholder model by Freeman quoted e.g. by Staffelbach:[25]

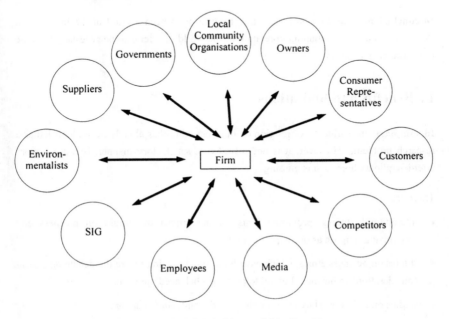

Illustration 4. Stakeholder model by Freeman

It clearly demonstrates that there is a need for the balancing of different interests: it is not only the shareholders who have to be taken into account. Unfortunately, the weakness of this model is that trade-offs have to be made between the interests involved.

Donaldson suggests a dual approach to ethics: on the one hand, he establishes the idea of a contract between corporation and society not unlike that employed by Rousseau and

---

[23] Please refer to footnote 20.

[24] Wilson (1993).

[25] Staffelbach (1994).

Hobbes for the relation between the individual and society. On the other hand he develops a concept of fundamental human rights.[26]

Nevertheless it is questionable whether this approach is truly applicable in Europe and the Muslim world without any modifications as most of the ideas on which it is based are linked to Western tradition.

In conclusion, studies on business ethics have to often been a proof of the impact of a Western or indeed Christian interpretation of the world. It seems to be necessary to come to a more balanced view.

E. Benefits and limitations

In summary, the influence of religion on business ethics has already been identified as a research problem. However, it is not solved in a satisfactory manner, because a more interdisciplinary approach is missing.

There are

- intercultural studies, providing hints on the impact of culture on business and recognising religion as one aspect of culture,
- studies on business ethics, which have for a long time dominated the debate on ethical considerations in business but fail to provide a balanced view, and
- studies on religions, showing how close Christianity and Islam are.

In order to work on the research questions, it is necessary to combine a theological and a business studies approach.

Therefore, in the following chapter, theoretical concepts about Muslim and Christian religion as well as about different ways to operate businesses are presented and referred to each other. This is preceded by a definition of the terms "Europe" and the "Muslim World".

---

[26] Donaldson (1989, 47).

CHAPTER III.

THEORETICAL STUDY:
FINDINGS, ANALYSIS, SYNTHESIS AND EVALUATION

A. Definition of "Europe" and the "Muslim World"

The **"Muslim World"** as referred to in this thesis consists of member countries of the Islamic Development Bank in which a population of more than 50 % are Muslims. These countries are distributed over four different geographical zones: the Near and Middle East including Turkey, Africa, the Indian Subcontinent including Afghanistan and Kyrghyzstan and finally Southeast Asia:[27]

- The **16 African countries** of the Muslim world are Algeria, Chad, Comoros, Djibouti, Egypt, Gambia, Guinea, Libya, Mali, Mauritania, Morocco, Niger, Senegal, Somalia, Sudan and Tunisia. The total population is 201,539,000.[28]

- The **14 countries in the Near and Middle East** belonging to the Muslim World are Bahrain, Iran, Iraq, Jordan, Kuwait, Lebanon, Oman, Qatar, Saudi Arabia, Syria, Turkey, Turkmenistan, United Arab Emirates and the Yemen. Population totals 206,045,000.[29]

- There are **five countries on the Indian Subcontinent, including Afghanistan and Kyrghyzstan**: Afghanistan, Bangladesh, Kyrghyzstan, Maldives and Pakistan. They have 260,548,000 inhabitants.

- Finally, there are **three Southeast Asian countries**, Brunei, Indonesia and Malaysia. Their total population is 206,472,000.

---

[27] Cf. von Baratta (1995).

[28] Benin, Burkina Faso, Cameroon, Gabon, Guinea-Bissau, Sierra Leone and Uganda are also members of the Islamic Development Bank, but Muslim population of these countries is less than 50 %.

[29] Khazakstan is not member of the Islamic Development Bank, but Muslim population of this country is more than 50 %.

There are also two European countries, Albania and Azerbaijan. The PLO is also a member. The following maps provide a good overview of the different regions of the Muslim World:[30]

Illustration 5. Muslim countries in Africa

---

30 : member country of the Islamic Development Bank of the respective region.

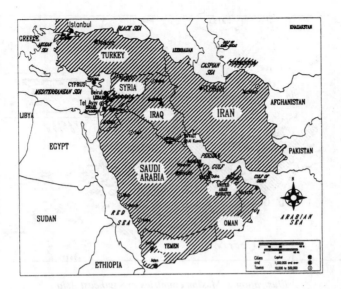

Illustration 6. Muslim countries in the Near and Middle East

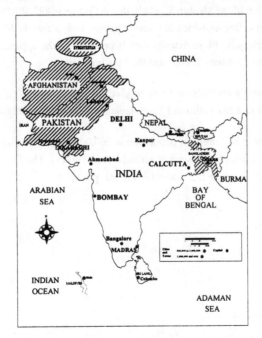

Illustration 7. Muslim countries on the Indian Subcontinent

Illustration 8. Muslim countries in Southeast Asia

The total population of the Muslim World in this definition is 885,386,000 if one includes the two European countries which are also countries with a mainly Muslim population, Albania and Azerbaijan. More detailed data is provided in the appendices, containing a numeric comparison between Europe and the Muslim World.

It is hardly impossible for the time being to give any details on Ex-Yugoslavia. For this research, all states that have followed Yugoslavia since its collapse are excluded.

In comparison, the total European population is 660,000,000 if **"Europe"** is taken in its largest definition, excluding Albania, Azerbaijan and Turkey. The following map shows Europe in the sense in which it is understood in this project:[31]

---

31 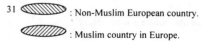 : Non-Muslim European country.

     : Muslim country in Europe.

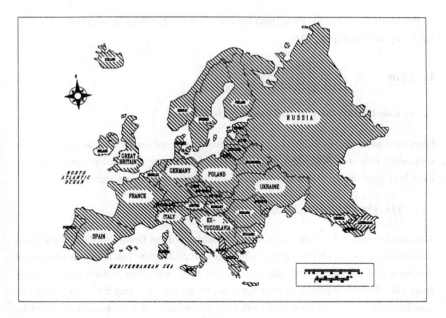

Illustration 9. Europe

For the purpose of this research which tackles a global issue, Europe is seen as one entity as opposed to another region of the world, the Muslim World. This implies ignoring the enormous differences between the different parts of Europe such as the countries of Catholic, Eastern Orthodox or Protestant tradition. This is of course a very important simplification.

This research will concentrate on central Western European countries, i.e. Great Britain, France, Germany and Switzerland.[32]

---

[32] A more detailed appreciation of the differences within Europe is provided on page 24. The differences between Catholicism, Protestantism and Eastern Orthodoxy will be explained in more detail on page 46.

Arabic terms are explained throughout the text. In the appendices, an overview of Arabic terms is provided on page 131.

1. Islam

a) Constituent elements and history of Islam

Islam is a monotheistic religion. "Islam" means "submission to God in peace". It is sometimes forgotten that Islam does not mean fatalism or denial of progress: Man is thought to have responsibility and is encouraged to reflect and to act accordingly.[33]

(1) The foundation

The foundation is the Koran, received by Mohammed of the Quraych tribe and the Banu Has-him clan. He was born in 570 CE, probably on 20 August. His father died before he was born, and his grandfather who took care of him, died when Mohammed was eight years old. Thus he experienced both death and loving care at a very early age. When he was 20 years of age, he started to work very successfully as a businessman. Soon he married one of the richest and nicest women in town according to reports of the time. He started to have revelations at the age of 40.[34]

The beginning of the Islamic era is dated to 622 CE when Mohammed moved out of Mecca and settled 280 miles to the north in Medina.[35] When he died at the age of 62, Islam had become a movement involving the creation of a special type of community with a specific government, laws and institutions.

Islam spread out during two great Arab dynasties, the Omayyad Caliphate (661-750 CE) and the Abbasid Caliphate (750-1258 CE). The later ended with the Mongol invasions, and it was only in the 16th century that most of the Muslim world was united in the Ottoman Empire in the Near and Middle East and the Mughal Empire in India. The Ottoman Empire lasted until the 1920s.[36]

---

[33] Le Gai Eaton (1994, 9-10).

[34] Le Gai Eaton (1994, 179-197).

[35] In Arab, *medina* means "city". Medina was originally called Yatrib. Only after the foundation of Islam, it became "the" city.

[36] Compare Oxford Analytica (1986, 9).

(2) The Koran

As Muslims think that the Koran is literally God's word, doctrine holds that it cannot be translated. Therefore, even a new English translation is called "The Meaning of the Glorious Koran".[37] This underlines the difference that exists for Muslims between revelation and inspiration: revelation is beyond human intelligence and its limitations, whereas inspiration enlightens intelligence without eliminating its limitations.

This perception of the Koran, the link of the meaning of the Koran and the Arabic language, i.e. contents and form, are due to the nature of the Arabic language: As it is based on three-character-roots and all words are derivatives of those roots, there are words in the Arabic language that apparently are not related at all, and still share the same root. This system, which is close to Hebrew and all other Semitic languages, has for instance been described by Le Gai Eaton.[38]

The Koran reports that there is only one God, who created the world and who forgives the sins of man. Furthermore, Islam recognises biblical personalities such as Abraham, Moses, Mary and Jesus. Mohammed was the founder of a new social and political order.[39]

Muslims think that the Koran is the most perfect of God's revelations to man. They call Mohammed the "Seal of the Prophets", although the orthodox Islamic teaching does not attribute him with divinity and emphasise that he is a human being. It is the Koran which has divine qualities.[40]

(3) The different denominations

There are mainly two denominations in Islam: the more orthodox and more numerous Sunnis on one hand and the Shi'is on the other hand. The principal dispute between the two is on who succeeded Mohammed as leader or *Imam* of the Muslim community. For the Sunnis, it passed to the first four orthodox Caliphs before it was continued in the Omayyad and Abbasid Caliphates (661-1258).

---

[37] Cf. Schimmel (1990, 28).

[38] Le Gai Eaton (1994, 140-144).

[39] Cf. Roux (1981, 191).

[40] Oxford Analytica (1986, 11).

The Shi'is' view of Islamic history is that Mohammed's son-in law Ali was the direct successor of Mohammed as leader, and that his descendants represent a line of rightful leaders. Most of the Shi'is are convinced that the twelfth leader of this line, Mohammed al-Mahdi, disappeared in 873 and believe that he did not die but became invisible. He is attributed final authority and will return to establish justice and Islamic rule in the world. Meanwhile, the interpreters of the law or *Mujtahidun* and the Mullahs hold religious authority.[41]

As a result of their different perception of Islamic history, Sunnis believe that political authority who succeeded Mohammed had only temporal power, while the Shi'is hold that the Hidden Imam has infallibility in the interpretation of religious truth. Therefore, while Sunnis have been ready to accept deficiencies of political power, the Shi'is are suspicious towards temporal political power.

b) Islamic ethics

The Koran puts great emphasis on jurisdiction and sociology. This should not lead to the somewhat sweeping assertion that there is nothing else. Indeed, some researchers report that Islam has been regarded as "scout-religion":[42] Islam is understood as a set of scout-like rules. For a Muslim, however, ethical behaviour is not a goal in its own right but a means to live his relation with God and his neighbour. Belief automatically leads to action and putting into practice human and spiritual values.

There are two main attitudes that are requested: sincerely worshipping God or *ikhlas*, and good behaviour towards one's neighbour or *ihsan*. God knows the limits of man and does not request more than man can do (Koran 2:286). Thus, Islam helps trusting in ones capacities which are to be enlarged through spiritual teaching.[43] Furthermore, Muslim doctrine defines five acts of worship, which are frequently referred to as the Five Pillars of Islam: the confession, the alms tax or *zakat*, the month of fasting or *ramadan*, the pilgrimage to Mecca and the prayer.[44]

---

[41] Oxford Analytica (1986, 12-14).

[42] Le Gai Eaton (1994, 34).

[43] Cf. Roux (1981, 198).

[44] For the following description of the five pillars of Islam, Schimmel (1990, 32-37) has provided very valuable information.

(1) The confession

Those who confess, that "there is no God but God, and Mohammed is his prophet" are the supporters of Islam. This confession or *shahada* cannot be found in the Koran word for word, and a longer confession results from a long development based on the Koran.

The first half of this confession expresses the monotheism of God. Muslims insist that the second half of the confession is what makes Islam unique: there are many people who believe that there is only one God, but Mohammed provides the practical applications. Following him means doing God's will.

(2) The alms tax

The alms tax or *zakat* tries to impose a fair taxation of the rich for the benefit of the poor. It has been interpreted as an alternative to capitalism and communism. This point will be dealt with in more detail later on page 40.

(3) The month of fasting

Despite of the fact that this is a difficult thing to do, it is probably the most widely practised rule. During the whole month of fasting or *ramadan*, which is the 9th month of the Islamic calendar of 354 days, eating, drinking, smoking and sex are forbidden from dawn to dusk. Each morning, the intention to fast has to be formulated. People who are exempted from fasting are travellers, pregnant and ill persons. They have to make up later or do something as a replacement. The month of fasting ends with celebrations during which gifts are exchanged.

(4) The pilgrimage to Mecca

This pilgrimage or *hajj* has to be done at a specific time, at least once during a Muslim's lifetime: the last month of the moon calendar. It should only be undertaken if the pilgrim is healthy and the family is in security and free of debt. The encounter of Muslims of very different background certainly strengthens the Muslim community.

(5) The prayer

The prayer or *slat* has to be performed five times per day. This number is not mentioned in the Koran, but it was probably the same even in Mohammed's time. It has been described as "the border between belief and unbelief". There is a specific sequence of gestures that go with the prayer. Muslims are called to the prayer into the mosques, but they can also pray alone. If the prayer takes place in a mosque, a Moslem has to wash himself according to strict rules. If there is no water, sand may be used instead. Friday is not a "day of rest" as Sunday is in the Christian tradition, but a day for communal prayer. In many Muslim countries, shops close and there is no school for the children.[45]

Even if a Muslim neglects one or more pillars, except for the first one, he would still be considered as supporter of Islam. However, if he denies their necessity, he would not be seen as such any more.[46] One would be correct in summing Islamic ethics up in two key elements: trust in God or *tawakkul* and mutual social responsibility.

c) Islamic business ethics

Islam accepts two forms of enrichment of the individual: labour and natural resources on one hand, and exchange, remittance of rights, outright grants and inheritance on the other.

(1) The concept of property

The cause of all property is God, who has distributed it to men to a varying extent. The rich are asked to give parts of their property to the poor, because they only act on God's behalf.[47]

As mentioned above, one of the five fundamental duties of a Muslim is the alms tax or *zakat*. This is widely accepted. The traditional basis for taxation are agricultural products such as fruit, raisins and sheep. The state has to manage the incoming money and to distribute it: to the poor, those who are dealing with them, prisoners, debtors, those who fight for Islam and travellers (Koran 9:60):[48]

> "Alms are for the poor and the needy, and those employed to administer the [funds]; for those whose hearts have been [recently] reconciled [to the truth]; for those in bondage and in debt; in the cause of ALLAH; and for the wayfarer: [thus is it] ordained by ALLAH, and ALLAH is full of knowledge and wisdom."

In addition to the formal duty of *zakat* there is the moral duty of donations or *sadaqa* to the family, orphans, the poor, travellers, beggars and prisoners (Koran 2:177):

---

[45] Klöcker, Tworuschka and Tworuschka (1995, 23).

[46] Cf. Le Gai Eaton (1994), Oxford Analytica (1986, 10) and Haarmann (1995, 117).

[47] Klöcker, Tworuschka and Tworuschka (1995, 31).

[48] All quotations of the Koran follow the text of The Meaning of the Holy Qur'àn (1995), the standard translation and commentary by Abdullah Yusuf Ali.

> "It is not righteousness that ye turn your faces towards East or West; but it is righteousness to believe in ALLAH and the Last Day, and the Angels and the book, and the messengers; to spend out of your substance, out of love for him, for your kin, for orphans, for the needy, for the wayfarer, for those who ask, and for the ransom of slaves ..."

Poverty is not blessed in Islam, however, the rich have more difficulties in obtaining salvation. That is because property is transitory (Koran 18:44, 27:36, 57:19), does not lead to men's immortality (Koran 104:3) and does not help during the final judgement (Koran 26:88, 58:18). The Koran holds that property as well as children only incite the desire to have more and meanwhile to forget God (30:28, 89:21, 90:6). The Koran gives a different perspective (24:36-38):

> "... By men [is He glorified] whom neither traffic nor merchandise can divert from remembrance of ALLAH, nor from regular prayer, nor from the practice of regular charity ..."

(2) The concept of labour

Because of its holistic approach to the human being, any occupation is worship. Therefore, work in the strict economic sense was not a religious issue in classic Islam. Work is not seen as a punishment for men's sins. The Koran distinguishes between God's creating and men's working and a Muslim would not try to imitate God in his working. It is more an activity in God's service.[49]

Since the 1930s, Muslim activists have developed specific working ethics. Labour was defined as an obligation to all who are able to work. There were also views that women should receive the same pay for the same type of work and that exploitation should be forbidden because of the Koran (4:32 and 7:42):

> "... to men is allotted what they earn, and to women what they earn ..."

> "... no burden we place on any soul, but that which it can bear ..."

Some thought that an ideal society would be installed if the following came into being (Koran 6:132):

> "To all are degrees [or ranks] according to their deeds: for thy LORD is not unmindful of anything that they do."

Strikes are only permitted if they oppose a company which in turn opposes the Islamic community.

---

[49] Klöcker, Tworuschka and Tworuschka (1995, 21-22).

(3) The concept of the environment

Within the Islamic World, a comprehensive discussion on environmental ethics has not started. This may be due to the fact that in many Muslim countries, development questions are ranked higher in importance than the question of the preservation of nature.

The Koran (7:54-7:56) tells that God has created the world and entitled man to rule over it under certain conditions. A Muslim is encouraged to act according to God's commandments as follows:

> "Your Guardian-LORD is ALLAH, who created the heavens and the earth in six days, then He established himself on the throne [of authority]: he draweth the night as a veil o'er the day, each seeking the other in rapid succession: he created the moon, and the stars, [all] governed by laws under his command. Is it not His to create and to govern? Blessed be ALLAH, the Cherisher and sustainer of the worlds!
>
> Call on your LORD with humility and in private: for ALLAH loveth not those who trespass beyond bounds.
>
> Do not mischief on the earth, after it hath been set in order, but call on Him with fear and longing [in your hearts]: for the mercy of ALLAH is [always] near those who do god."

God remains the true governor, even if man has the temporary right to use the world's resources. Islamic protection of the environment is not only motivated by human need, but also by respect towards the creator.

(4) The historic Muslim approach to exchange and trade

As the Muslim world grew rapidly after Mohammed's death in 632 CE, it brought together two enormous economic areas which had been divided politically for a long time. On one hand the Mediterranean basin with the routes to Africa and points of access to European raw materials. The second area regrouped the lands around the Indian Ocean as well as Iraq, Iran and Central Asia. This lead to a boost in business activities which reached a peak in the ninth century.[50]

There is no doubt that the Islamic tradition has always included a positive approach to economic activity, Mohammed being himself a merchant before his prophetic mission.

---

[50] Oxford Analytica (1986, 17-18).

(5) The payment of interest

The Koran does not allow the payment of *riba* (Koran 2:275).[51] There are two possible interpretations:

Liberal Muslims think that *riba* does not mean the relatively modest interest of today's banks, but only about excessive usury. They would argue that the idea behind the interdiction of *riba* is to avoid exploitation of one Muslim by another, and to avoid gains without due effort of work.[52] This can be related back on the limitation of ethically accepted forms of enrichment.[53]

It may be asserted, however, that the dominant and increasingly popular interpretation is that *riba* means any interest payment. Interest is seen as

1. a way of arbitrarily creating new capital without corresponding increase in the supply of goods. In an Islamic economic system, new capital is to be created from real commercial transactions only. Therefore, inflationary tendencies are reduced.
2. unjustified and unethical burden for future generations to pay in the case of public sector borrowing. Only asset-based financing is permissible, therefore limiting public sector borrowing to the acquisition of assets and forcing governments to limit their current expenditure to the national resources available to them.[54]

In consequence, Islamic banks tend to involve a borrower in profits and losses of companies in which the bank is investing.[55] Thus, there is no fixed rate but a return based on real commercial activity.

It was Umar who expressed the difficulties of the interpretation of *riba* because Mohammed died before this question was clarified.[56]

---

[51] Oxford Analytica 1986, 18, refers to the fact that the Arabic word *riba* is not to be confused with *ribh* which means profit and is not forbidden at all.

[52] Oxford Analytica (1986, 18).

[53] Cf. page 40.

[54] Pervez (1995).

[55] Haarmann (1995, 114).

[56] In The Meaning of the Holy Qur'àn (1995), it is pointed out that this was one of the three questions on which he would have liked to get more clarification from Mohammed. The two other questions were Khilafah and Kalalah in the context of inheritance law (Koran 4:12).

(6) The idea of an Islamic economic system

For some time now, Muslims have argued that a supreme Islamic economic system could be built. However, there is no simple answer as to what such a system would look like.[57]

Until the 1950s, support of private enterprise was often linked to a rejection of some Western business attitudes judged incompatible with Muslim beliefs. More radical interpretations have gained increasing support however. They are based on criticism of concentration of wealth and corruption that often comes with economic growth and an increasing influence of the West. These interpretations focus on anti-capitalistic views of Ali (d. 661), Mohammed's son-in-law, and of Umar (d. 644), who wanted to limit property-holding and wealth.[58]

Practical examples of Islamic economies vary significantly from one another: Saudi Arabia and Libya are not running their economies close to Koranic rulings, while Iran did not reform its system due to the political and military turmoils since 1979. The difficulties are based on the limited basis of explicit rule in the Koran and the Prophetic Traditions.

A central element of the Islamic economic system is the definition of money, which is traditionally seen as

1. a means of exchange,
2. a unit of value,
3. a store of value and
4. a medium of deferred value.

While functions 1. and 2. are accepted by Islamic economists, money is not seen as a store of value whose final worth is a function of the trend of prices. The reason is that money is only seen as a claim to a number of goods of commercial value to be purchased in the future. Therefore, money keeps transactions in abeyance and cannot be equated with goods for five reasons:[59]

1. Its owner obtains real income only by holding money, i.e. without exchanging it against goods,

---

[57] Cf. Nomani / Rahnema (1994).

[58] Oxford Analytica (1986, 32-33).

[59] Cf. Pervez (1995).

2. money is liquid and has only negligible carrying or production cost and cannot be substituted,

3. demand for money is only derived from the demand for goods that it can buy and is not genuine,

4. money does not depreciate as goods do,

5. money has no intrinsic value like goods but is merely a product of social convention.

If lending money is seen as a transfer of rights to purchase a number of goods in the future, then interest is outside the legitimate framework of individual property rights. This leads to a critical view of the payment of interest as being only a theoretical construct.

Within this argumentation, however, at least the perception of money as unit of value that does not depreciate (4.) is questionable. After all, there is inflation that has to be taken into account.

(7) The insurance sector

Another problem is the insurance sector. Muslims tend to think that it is close to banking with interest. Furthermore, it appears to be similar to gambling and puts into question one's trust in God.

2. Christianity

a) Constituent elements and history of Christianity

Like Muslims, Christians also share the conviction that there is one single God. Christian teaching also says that Jesus is the son of God, and that the holy spirit is the third part of the trinity, together with God the father and with the Holy Spirit.

(1) The foundation

The foundation is the Bible and the belief in the specific role of Jesus Christ as saviour of humanity. God has made an alliance with man and especially with Israel. According to Christian teaching, Jesus has saved the world and all human beings by means of his own death.

Pentecost is the day of the Holy Spirit which is the creation of the church. Christians share the belief that Jesus is the bases of their faith, and that there are two main sacraments or holy acts: baptism, the sign that a person enters the community of Christians, and the Eucharist, the remembrance of the last supper of Jesus before his death.

(2) The Bible

The Bible is the common ground of all Christians. It demonstrates the link between God and man, particularly with the people of Israel. It is divided into the Hebrew Bible or Old Testament, which was originally written in Hebrew and only later translated into Greek and Latin, and the New Testament, originally written in Greek.[60]

Among Christians, the Bible is widely seen as a human report of the history between God and men. Therefore it should be interpreted and translated. Versions in central European languages of the complete text came only into existence with the Reform in the XVIth century.

It reports that God has created the world, that Jesus, son of Mary of King David's family, has lived and taught in Palestine and thus continued the link between God and man. It also describes how the apostles founded the church. It shows that man is good and bad at the same time and that there are also degrees in-between.

(3) The different denominations

Today, the most important denominations in terms of numbers of supporters are Catholicism, Eastern Orthodoxy and Protestantism which all have their particularities.

Catholicism gives high esteem to the mother of Jesus, Mary. Also, the Catholic Church is organised around the Pope, who is seen not only as bishop of Rome, but also a spiritual leader of all Christians and top of the hierarchy of the Catholic Church.

It knows seven sacraments which are seen as means to obtain forgiveness for the sins. They are: baptism, confirmation, the Eucharist, penance, extreme unction, ordination and matrimony.[61]

---

[60] A part of the New Testament is supposed to have been written in Hebrew originally.

[61] Roux (1981, 17-58). Compare "Ecclesia semper reformanda est." [The church has to undergo constant reform.]

Eastern Orthodoxy keeps the tradition of the seven gatherings of all Christians, or oicumenical councils. Since the last such council in 787 CE, several important letters have contributed to Orthodox tradition. It puts great emphasis on the triangle of faith, tradition and liturgy.

The term "Eastern Orthodoxy" was introduced after the schism between the Greek and Latin Christian Churches of the Eastern and the Western part of the former Roman Empire. It has to be differentiated from Monophysite Churches, a term that is used for Eastern Churches that did not accept the Chalcedonian canons, such as the Coptic, Ethiopian, Armenian and Jacobite Churches.[62]

As far as its teaching is concerned, the Orthodox church is based on the power of the resurrection of Christ. It sees itself as church of the East, even though it is a church of a Western religion in terms of von Glasenapp.[63]

Protestantism has developed from the Catholic Church with Luther in Germany and Scandinavia and Calvin in the French speaking world and the Netherlands, while Zwingli influenced the German speaking part of Switzerland. The third part of the Protestant movement is the Anglican Church in England. In some countries, e. g. Germany, Protestants have for a long time been the majority of people. In other countries, e. g. France, they have always been a minority but obtained considerable influence in the respective society. The Protestant and the Catholic Church are both Western Churches as opposed to the Eastern Orthodox Church.

The key elements of Protestantism are that God is seen as only source of hope, God's grace as only way to obtain salvation and of the Bible as guiding principle of the Church.

Furthermore, the Holy Spirit is seen as source of inspiration, leading to the universal sacerdoce which underlines the responsibility that all Christians have for the spreading of the faith. The church is seen as in need for permanent reform with stress on the importance of the local community of Christians.[64]

---

[62] Cf. Brown (1993): Monophysite churches hold that Jesus is of one single nature. The ecumenical council of Chalcedon (451 CE) declared that in Jesus there is a devine and a human nature.

[63] Cf. von Glasenapp (1994), Roux (1981, 95-143).

[64] Cf. Roux (1981, 73-87).

b) Christian ethics

(1) The 10 commandments

Central to Christian teaching on ethics are the 10 commandments that can be extracted out of the Hebrew Bible in Exodus 20:2-20:17:[65]

1. (2) I am the LORD your God, who brought you out of Egypt, out of the land of slavery. (3) You shall have no other gods before me. (4) You shall not make for yourself an idol in the form of anything in heaven above or on the earth beneath or in the waters below. (5) You shall not bow down to them or worship them; for I, the LORD your God, am a jealous God, punishing the children for the sin of the fathers to third and fourth generation of those who hate me, (6) but showing love to those who love me and keep my commandments.

2. (7) You shall not misuse the name of the LORD your God, for the LORD will not hold anyone guiltless who misuses his name.

3. (8) Remember the Sabbath day by keeping it holy. (9) Six days you shall labour and do all your work, (10) but the seventh day is a Sabbath to the LORD your God. On it you shall not do any work, neither you, nor your son or daughter, not your manservant or maidservant, nor your animals, nor the alien within your gates. (11) For in six days the LORD made the heavens and the earth, the sea, and all that is in them, but he rested on the seventh day. Therefore the LORD blessed the Sabbath day and made it holy.

4. (12) Honor your father and your mother, so that you may live long in the land the LORD your God is giving you.

5. (13) You shall not murder.

6. (14) You shall not commit adultery.

7. (15) You shall not steal.

8. (16) You shall not give false testimony against your neighbour.

9. (17) You shall not covet your neighbour's house.

10. You shall not covet your neighbour's wife, or his manservant or maidservant, his ox or donkey, or anything that belongs to your neighbour.

(2) The commandment of love

In the New Testament, Jesus is reported to have reinforced the old law and focused it on two points that are equally written in the Hebrew Bible.[66] In Deuteronomy 6:5 it says:

"Love the LORD your God with all your heart and with all your soul and with all your strength."

---

[65] All translations of the Hebrew Bible follow The Interlinear NIV Hebrew-English Old Testament (1987).

[66] Cf. Matthew 22:36-22:40.

48

The second part is written in Leviticus 19:18:

> "Do not seek revenge or bear a grudge against one of your people, but love your neighbour as yourself."

Especially the second part of the commandment of love reinforced by Jesus has been misinterpreted as specifically Christian or as an opposition to the Old Testament. It has also been shortened to the famous "brotherly love".

(3) The basis of Christian humaneness

From these traditions, the basis of Christian humaneness has been deducted. It can be condensed to three key areas: faith, hope and love. It can be seen clearly that the first and the third one are deducted from the 10 commandments and the commandment of love. Hope is an intermediate between the two others and provides a link between the relation God-men on one side and men-men on the other.

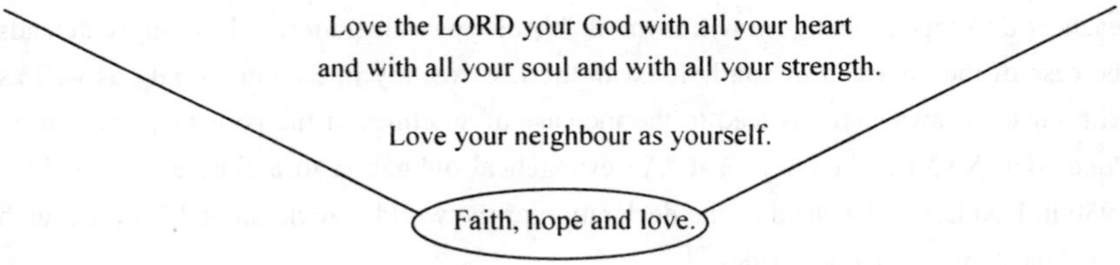

Love the LORD your God with all your heart
and with all your soul and with all your strength.

Love your neighbour as yourself.

Faith, hope and love.

Illustration 10. Christian ethics

(4) The mission

Christians are called to do missionary work, which has long-time been understood in Europe as teaching and baptising other people by force.[67] In the second half of this century, this understanding has become less aggressive and more concerned with the situation in the European countries themselves.

---

[67] Cf. Mark 15:15-15:16.

c) Christian business ethics

Arthur Rich has formulated two basic principles of Christian business ethics: business should be organised in a way that it serves human needs and that it is appropriate to the task.[68]

(1) The concept of property

Property has known very differing valuations: From fully accepting property and pro-tecting it by a legal system to warnings of property being an obstacle in following Jesus who was poor himself. The latter type of ethics could only be found with the first Christian parishes, the first monks and some laic movements. Poverty was regarded as an ideal of renunciation and concentration much like virginity and obedience. St. Thomas Aquinas judged property as reasonable if it was linked with the common welfare.[69]

As a reaction to the unbalanced distribution of property at a global scale, roman-catholic teachers developed what is now known as "theology of liberation". It strongly defends the case of the poor and of solidarity with the less wealthy in the community as well as with those far away. It has lead to the increase of an ethics of the poor as expressed by Pope John XXXIII, the encyclical "An evangelical obligation to a simple style of life" 1980 in Hoddeston, England or the declaration of the world church council "For a church of solidarity with the poor" 1980.[70]

(2) The concept of labour

In the Christian context, work is a divine mandate to continue God's creation on earth under the condition of sin. Over the centuries, thinking on the understanding of work has changed over and over again. In medieval times, monks of some holy orders were supposed not to work which lead to a contemptuous approach to work.

Luther and Calvin however underlined that all Christians are asked to believe and to work, and redefined the understanding of work itself. Under the influence of Pro-testantism, work and success became signs of God's election which in turn contributed to

---

[68] Cf. Rich 1990, 226-258.

[69] Klöcker, Tworuschka and Tworuschka (1995, 30).

[70] Klöcker, Tworuschka and Tworuschka (1995, 31).

the industrial revolution. Modern social ethics try to reconcile today's business life with the judgements of the Bible and the reformation.[71]

On the catholic side, the pope has dealt with the issue of justice in working conditions several times. In 1981, he judged the rights and interests of workers higher than those of the owners of the capital.

Although there are some differences, there is unanimity among Christian thinkers that there is a right to work, a human working environment, implication of the working people in the decision making process and the establishment of justice in the global economic system. In order to balance everyday work and stress, Christian thinkers recommend "rests" during which the relation to God is the centre of people's minds.[72]

(3) The concept of the environment

Following the massive destruction of nature, only recently a Christian environmental ethic has been developed. However, the concept of the environment has been central to the Christian faith from the beginning: God is seen as the creator of heaven and earth. He has given his instructions to men that can be found in the Hebrew Bible in Genesis 1:26-1:28:

> "Then God said: 'Let us make man in our image, in our likeness, and let them rule over the fish of the sea and the birds of the air, over the livestock, over all the earth, and over all the creatures that move along the ground.'
>
> So God created man in his own image, in the image of God he created him; male and female he created them.
>
> God blessed them and said to them, 'Be fruitful and increase in number; fill the earth and subdue it. Rule over the fish of the sea and the birds of the air and over every living creature that moves on the ground.'"

This has long been understood in the way that man is entitled by God to rule at his place. A part of the motivation of Western industrialised countries to use natural resources regardless of the consequences might be based here. Today, there is a growing consensus that ruling over nature should more be understood as in Genesis 2:15:

> "The LORD God took the man and put him in the Garden of Eden to work it and take care of it."

---

[71] Klöcker, Tworuschka and Tworuschka (1995, 19).

[72] Klöcker, Tworuschka and Tworuschka (1995, 20).

51

Churches today plea individually and on an oicumenical basis for a radical change in peoples consciousness. Even if differences can be found, there is a common concern for the protection of the environment.

(4) The payment of interest

There is a long Judaeo-Christian biblical tradition of prohibition of interest. In the Hebrew Bible, there are several examples:

> "If you lend money to any of My people with you who is poor, you shall be to him as a creditor, and you shall not exact interest from him." (Exodus 22:24)

> "If one of your countrymen becomes poor and is unable to support himself among you, help him as you would an alien or a temporary resident, so he can continue to live among you. Do not take interest of any kind from him, but fear your God, so that your countryman may continue to live among you. You must not lend him money or sell him food at a profit." (Leviticus 25:35-37)

> "To a foreigner you may lend upon interest, but to your brother you shall not." (Deuteronomy 23:21).

> "He that hath not given this money upon usury; nor taken reward against the innocent; he that doeth theses things shall never fall." (Psalm 15)

> "He that hath not given forth upon usury, neither hath taken any increase, that hath withdrawn his hand from iniquity, hath executed true judgement between man and man." (Ezekiel 18:8).

Deuteronomy 23:21 played an important role in medieval times, when Christians were not allowed to work as moneylenders, which was done by Jews. Jews were discredited as extortionate people who drive hard bargains.

In the New Testament, Jesus is quoted:

> "Love your enemies and do good; lend, expect nothing in return." (Luke 6:35)

On the other hand, in his parable in Matthew 25:14-30 he points out that one should use capital to maximise it and at least borrow it against payment of interest.

In the fourth century, when the Christian faith became the state religion of the late Roman Empire, clergy was forbidden from taking interest. Four centuries later, Charlemagne ruled that usury was a criminal offence. St. Thomas Aquinas thought extra payments for lending money to be unlawful. In 1311, Pope Clement V finally prohibited usury and declared any secular legislation in favour of usury null and void.[73]

---

[73] Pervez (1995).

52

In medieval times, the banking system was hold by Jews. Only towards the end of the sixteenth century did charging a reasonable level of interest became a generally accepted practice for Christians. In order to protect from excesses, authorities imposed maximum interest rates.

C. Two ethical modes of operations

Following the analysis of how ethical systems refer to business activities, this part well deal with the question how the two ethical modes of operations included in this research project work in theory. It serves as a basis for the empirical investigation in chapter 131

First, attention will be given to the concept of Islamic banking and insurance. Main attention will be given to the Islamic banking instruments being key to this type of banking. As a second step, the way in which co-operative banks and insurance companies work will be dealt with. It will be shown how the concepts for this mode of operation have developed over time.

In order to fully understand these two modes of operation, the reader is assumed to have general knowledge of conventional banking which consists of lending and borrowing money against interest payments within a business relation between a customer and a bank.

1. Islamic banking and insurance

First of all, instead of reasoning on a market interest rate, Islamic banking is based on the idea of a "market rate of return". Secondly, Islamic financial instruments are linked directly to the type of underlying asset. Four types of instruments can be differentiated:

1. Financial **claims for monetary value based on certain durable goods or property with a predictable income stream as a basis or *Ijara***. This type of instrument can be marketed and discounted since ownership of the instrument passes claims on goods and not debt.

2. **Similar claims but with an unpredictable income: *Modaraba* and traditional equities**. An evaluation takes place after a certain time. This type of instruments can be marketed but not discounted.

3. **Claims on income streams resulting from commercial transactions**. An evaluation takes place at certain intervals. There are no durable goods involved and discounting is not permitted.

4. **Claims concerning debts payable at certain future dates**. They may be traded at the face value but not discounted.

These instruments will now be described in greater depth.[74]

a) Claims based on goods with predictable income stream

Financial instruments of this type or *Ijara* mean the leasing of an asset under financial or operating aspects, to a third party for a specified time. There is a permanent revenue stream creating return on top of the depreciation cost of the asset.

Fixed rental leading to fixed income is possible as well as variable rental that is to be revised at certain intervals, thereby creating a variable or "floating" income. *Ijara* represents ownership of goods. Discounts and premiums are legitimate, because goods can be freely bought and sold between free parties.

b) Claims based on goods with unpredictable income stream

As far as *modaraba* is concerned, this instrument means a claim against a fund or *modaraba*, managed by an Islamic bank quite similar to investment trust units or mutual funds in the Western system.

In the case of an unrestricted *modaraba*, the bank is authorised to manage the affairs of the fund on its own responsibility, including selling and buying property, appointing one or more agents to buy and sell on its behalf and safe-keeping, renting and hiring the assets.

In the case of a restricted *modaraba*, the bank is limited to a period, place, purpose and type of business as specified in the *modaraba* agreement. The bank is not allowed to mix its own property with the fund's assets or appoint agents.

---

[74] For the following part, Pervez (1996) has provided very valuable information.

The main characteristics of *modaraba* are:

1. Asset valuation takes place at the end of the period.
2. If a net loss occurs, the net asset value is reduced while the bank loses its management fees.
3. Creditors cannot access the other assets of the investment holders if these claims exceed the total assets of the *modaraba*.
4. The bank's management fee may be a fixed percentage of the net profits, but not a fixed amount.
5. A reserve for unforeseen losses may be built, which is distributed to the holders when all the costs and claims are met.
6. *Modaraba* may only be traded if at least 51 % of the total assets are tangible assets.

Investment in traditional national and international equities is permitted if the companies are not involved in trading and/or producing prohibited items including intoxicating substances, items of an obscene nature, destructive weapons, interest-based institutions or insurance companies.

As there are virtually no companies in the developed world without interest-based debt, Islamic scholars accept them as part of the funds if a portion of the profits, e.g. 10 to 15 %, are given away as charity.

c) Claims on income streams resulting from commercial transactions

This instrument is close to the marketable *modaraba*, but discounts or premiums are prohibited. As the underlying tangible assets are less than 51 % of the total assets, this instrument is considered a debt even though the assets may represent concluded commercial transactions. It can be considered for placement of surplus money between banks through the interbank market as well as through deposit certificates.

d) Claims concerning debts payable at certain future dates

In the case of *modaraba*, this instrument is a monetary claim to obtain a sum of money within an underlying commercial transaction. The bank buys items from a client at his request and sells it back to the client on spot, or at a later point in time at a higher price. The price difference represents the transaction profit. Normally, this instrument is a short term solution, although it may be used as a long-term instrument, if the underlying assets are durable goods and both parties agree on a long-term relationship. There is a fixed pre-determined rate of return to the bank which brings it close to interest payments. However, there is always an initiating economic activity, i.e. the movement of goods. The Koran (2:275) clearly underlines the difference from a religious perspective:

> "Those who devour usury will not stand except as stands one whom the evil one by his touch hath driven to madness. That is because they say: 'Trade is like usury', but ALLAH hath permitted trade and forbidden usury. ..."

Islamic banks tend to use *modaraba* to manage their liquidity through sale of goods and purchase of deferred payment agreements. Discounting is not permitted, because this is mainly a debt instrument.

In the case of *salam*, or advance payment, this instrument is a claim against a client who promises to deliver precisely specified goods at a specified time and place in the future. If he is not able to deliver on time, he has to return the payment, but without any additional charges. As in the case described under 4.1., discounting is not permitted.

In the case of *istisna*, this instrument is a claim against a manufacturer for the production and supply of precisely specified goods. The bank may or may not pay in advance. The paper representing *istisna* can be bought and sold at its face value.

A purely monetary claim against the client issuing the debt document is called *qard hassan*. It is used to provide interest-free financial aid to an existing client who is in temporary financial difficulties. The debt has to be repaid, because non-payment would damage the welfare of society at large.

e) Islamic insurance

As conventional insurance was found to violate the *Shariah* concepts, leading Islamic scholars and legal experts worked out a new type of contract which claims to be in accordance with *Shariah* law. The result was the concept of Islamic insurance or *takafol*.

2. Co-operative banking and insurance

The co-operative financial system is based on a balance between mutual support and self-help. One of the most important promoters of this system in Europe was **Friedrich Wilhelm Raiffeisen** (1818-1888).[75]

In the early 1830s, the industrial revolution came into the villages and smaller towns in Germany and tradesmen were challenged by industrial production. It was extremely difficult to obtain a credit from one of the newly founded industry's banks which was necessary in order to buy machines. Therefore, they had to accept money from traders and usurers.

The problems of the rural population culminated in the famine in 1846/47. Raiffeisen founded a charity to help the poor immediately. In 1864 he started to replace benevolent donations to the poor rural population by financial institutes which provide capital to those who would not be able to produce any securities and who would otherwise depend on usury.

Independently but at the same time, **Hermann Schulze** created a help fund in Delitzsch in Saxony. He also noticed, that charity does not solve the problem in the longer term and therefore also established co-operatives, amongst which the *Vorschußverein für Tischler und Schuhmacher* founded in 1850 and the *Dahrlehenskasenverein zu Eilenburg* in the following year. It would later become the model for the *Volksbanken* or people's banks.

His institutes provided credit to rescue the tradesmen and their independence. As many people as possible were encouraged to become members and to sign at least one of the relatively small parts.[76]

In the co-operative system, there are no customers but members who either provide money or receive credit from other members. Operations are controlled by the general assembly of the members. A second principle that increases security is the rule that all operations have to be done by two people: the clerk and a second person who controls all operations involving money and keeps copies of all books.

---

[75] Maxeiner, Aschhoff, Wendt (1988) provide an introduction in his biography.

[76] More ample information is provided in Maxeiner, Aschhoff and Wendt (1988).

Raiffeisen formulated the principles of co-operative banking in a book that became a standard reference in this domain.[77] He also became the editor of a journal in which he promoted his ideas. Co-operative banking was first incorporated in Germany's law in 1867.

In the years following the victory over France in 1871, the co-operatives took part in the economic upturn. Today's legislation is based on the 1889 version "Gesetz betreffend die Erwerbs- und Wirtschaftsgenossenschaften".[78]

Muhammad Yunus (1941-) contributed largely to the development op co-operative banking in Asia since the 1970s. Originally a professor of economics at Chittagong University, he suffered from the gap between economic development theories he was teaching and the reality of the Bangladesh famine of 1974.

During field observations in 1976 he noticed that the main problem of the poor was the lack of working capital: the poor had to borrow money from traders at excessive interest rates which forced them to sell the result of their labour at any price just to be able to pay back the credit. He provided it from his own money, and also tried to establish a link between the poor and the bank in the village he observed. The beginning was difficult, because the bank asked collateral, which the poor could not provide. Only when he provided himself as guarantor the bank agreed. He only obtained money when he offered himself to guarantee for the credit and had excellent pay-back rates. As the banks would still not accept credit for the poor as their business, he established a bank for the poor himself.

Yunus elaborated very strict rules for co-operative banking in order to reduce the risk of unpaid debts. However, he based co-operative banking on the ideas of flexibility, self-reliance and identification of members with the bank, because these members participate in founding the bank, in defining rules and regulations, in savings mobilisation and in credit management.

An important element of his concept was the attention he was giving to women as potential clients. He thought of them as being more reliable as debtors than men for two reasons: because of a greater focus on long-term goals and because credit is the most important instrument for the empowerment of women because it gives them means that the otherwise lack.

---

[77] Raiffeisen (1866).

[78] (GenG), published in Reichsgesetzblatt I, 55.

The principles of a co-operative bank in Yunus's definition are:

- delivery of credit is main activity,

- credit is delivered at the doorstep,

- credit is provided exclusively to the poor (women),

- loans must be used only for income generating activities,

- potential borrowers are trained and tested,

- there is close supervision and savings are compulsory,

- transaction cost are kept as low as possible,

- staff is rigorously trained,

- no collateral or guarantee is requested,

- procedures are simple,

- banking centres are self-elected and village-based,

- there is (a plan for) institutionalisation, bank has NGO status and is politically neutral,

- the borrower initiates a social development program,

- repayments are small.

D. Synthesis and evaluation of theory

Europe and the Muslim World

With a total population of the Muslim World of 885,386,000 and a population of 660,000,000 in Europe, two environments if similar size are compared in this research. It is important to note that both terms are used as geographical terms throughout this report.

Islam and Christianity

As far as the **foundations** of the respective religions, the Bible and the Koran, are concerned, a difference in perception exists: While Christians widely see the Bible as a human report of the history between God and man, Muslims think that the Koran is God's word: They hold that it is was revealed to Mohammed word by word. There is however a common approach in that theologians of both religions read the respective texts in the original languages in order to better understand them.

In terms of **ethics**, Christianity and Islam are surprisingly close: while Islam asks its supporters to sincerely worship God and to behave well towards the neighbour, Christianity defines the love of God and the love of the neighbour as the highest commandments. Both religions tend to be exclusive and all-encompassing.

Ethics referring to business in general and particularly to banking differ. The concepts have changed over time: within Europe, the general conviction has moved at the end of medieval times from forbidding interest as remuneration of the lender to allowing it while only abusive interest or usury would not be accepted. Meanwhile, in the Muslim World of today interest is less and less accepted, be it abusive or not. This statement is supported by the growing importance of Islamic banking and insurance.

Islamic and Co-operative banking

When analysing the **two modes of operation**, it was found out that they are particular in the business they accept, i.e. in the kind of products they offer, and in their organisation.

The key elements of Islamic banking are the *Islamic financial instruments* which will be described in the following. Islamic Banking concentrates on the aspect of remuneration of the lender. It replaces the concept of debt finance based on interest by a system of profit sharing. The organisation is similar to those of conventional banks. Islamic Banking can be described as based on an ethic of convictions.

On the other hand, it is the *organisation* which is key to co-operative banking. It focuses on the allocation of credit. It replaces a system which provides credit to those who do already possess a lot by an alternative that provides credit to the poor who desperately need it. Financial instruments are similar to those of conventional banks. Co-operative banking can therefore be described as based on an ethic of responsibility.

Islamic financial instruments

There are instruments for the **gathering of funds**, namely *non-marketable modaraba* which are certificates of deposits and *takafol* deposits which correspond to insurance policies. The later are managed by *takafol* companies.

On the other hand, there are a number of **funds-channelling** products:
- *Ijara-Wa-Iktina*, corresponding to lease purchase, and *ijara* or leasing,
- *istisna* or finance of manufacturing, *salam* or advance payment sale,
- *morabaha* or sale and resale, which is the alternative to conventional interest-based loans,
- *qard hassan* or interest-free loans, which are emergency funds, and finally
- *asset-based modaraba*. The later, which is participation financing, can be unrestricted or restricted to certain projects only. A variation is *musharaka* or mutual participation financing, in which case the bank invests some of its own capital, too.

Co-operative financial organisation

Co-operative banking means a change in business processes. There is no customer-bank relationship as in conventional banking, but a relationship between members adhering to and thus forming a bank. As the members are often, at least in the early life of a bank, the less privileged, co-operative banking is a system of mutual help.

CHAPTER IV.

PLANS, METHODS AND MEANS OF RESEARCH

A. Need for a research method

If research is understood as the interpretation of signs in order to formulate general laws and as production of new clues in order to verify theses laws, it is essential to refer to an explicit research method.

This research method consists of all practices and operations which the researcher uses to make observations, and of the rules by which theses observations can be modified and interpreted in order to asses their meaning as clues. Without reflection, research can become an activity influenced by numerous prejudices.[79]

B. Research method used for this project

After the **definition of the research problem**, which is to establish the extend to which the structures of sample religions influence business ethics in a representative sample which is in this case banking, the **exploration** of existing scientific work has shown that it provides little help.

As a next step, the relevant elements of the project, i.e. the two environments, the two religions and their respective ethical systems, and the two modes of operations were analysed in a **theoretical study**. Thus, the aspects of the business that can be observed and related to the supposed influence, were established.

The following logical step is now to investigate in the current practices of Islamic banking in Europe and the Muslim World, and similarly in the practice of co-operative banking in both environments, in an **empirical study**:

Hypothesis is that an independent variable has an effect on a dependent variable: The effect of religion on business ethics is to be studied. The *experiment* is to measure the

---

[79] Cf. Alasuutari (1995).

63

type of business accepted and the way to operate within the same economic sector, in an experiment group of companies that does explicitly refer to religion and tries to follow an ethical concept, and in a control group of companies that does not explicitly refer to religion but still has an ethical concept.[80]

When *defining and coding the variables*, the objective is the reduction of the potential amount of observations into a more manageable number.[81] The independent variable is "religion", and the dependent variable is "business ethics", measured by the business accepted and the way to operate. In addition, there is an *intervening variable*, which is the environment: Europe and the Muslim World. These environments are dominated by differing religions with differing ethical systems.

In order to produce *general laws*, all companies in the experiment group registered with the Institute of Islamic Banking and Insurance, London, could be contacted. As the control group is too large to include every institution, a representative sample is taken by contacting only a limited number of institutions in both environments.

A way to obtain information at reasonable cost in limited time had to be found. Written interviews appeared most promising. In general, interviews that focus on the aspect of transfer of information can be differentiated from those that focus on the relation between the two partners. Within this research project, the group of interviewed people consisted of experts only, from whom information had to be obtained. In this case, the selected method of written interviews provided the best potential.[82]

Before collecting data, the *design of the questionnaire* was essential. It asks only questions of interest for the research and that are essential from the point of view of the research design. A standardised procedure promised the best results because it would produce information that could be compared most easily.[83] Alternative answers were pre-defined. In order to give room to information that was not included into the theoretical concepts one might have thought of, some open questions were also included.

---

[80] Cf. Alasuutari (1995).

[81] Cf. Bortz (1988).

[82] Van Koolwijk (1974, 15 and 146).

[83] Cf. Spöhring (1989).

C. Design of the questionnaire

The main question is: "What should we look for to differentiate Christian and Muslim influences in business?" This is divided in a part on background information, followed by information on operations and an evaluation and outlook.

In order to deal best with the differences that exist between co-operative and Islamic banking, two versions of questionnaires were established. They are very similar, but take into account the specialities of the relevant system. In the appendices, samples of the questionnaires are provided.

1. Background information

First of all, general information on the institutes should be collected, including the number of branches, the date of formation and the structure of ownership. As far as the background of Islamic banking is concerned, the objective was to assess to which point Islamic principles are incorporated in the state's law. In addition it was interesting to see who founded the banks and manages them today. Also it would be good to gain insight in the relevance of religious and other supervisory boards.

2. Information on operations

The aim of this part was to look into the practice of lending and borrowing money. How is the prohibiting of interest payments according to religious law interpreted and applied in Islamic banks? Are there any differences between the Islamic and the co-operative operations? Furthermore, it was necessary to find out whether there are any particularly religious business attitudes in both groups of banks. Typical Islamic business attitudes might include observing ritual prayers, or business might by conducted differently during the month of fasting. Typical Christian attitudes might include an orientation towards general welfare.

3. Financial evaluation and outlook

Finally, it would be very helpful to obtain information on the capital structure, the economic performance and future plans of the companies included in the research. This would allow to say whether companies are not only able to comply to religious laws but also to market pressure.

At the end, **findings** were interpreted in order to obtain **results**. Reference to other research and hypotheses was established.

CHAPTER V.

EMPIRICAL STUDY:
FINDINGS, ANALYSIS, SYNTHESIS AND EVALUATION

A. Hypotheses

Based on the theoretical findings, a number of hypotheses were formulated. They were condensed into the following four:

1. Hypothesis: There is a direct influence of Islam on Islamic banks in the Muslim World and in Europe, which is expressed in the business accepted by the banks and in the way they operate.

2. Hypothesis: There is an indirect influence of Christian Faith on co-operative banks in Europe and a similarly indirect influence of Islam on co-operative banks in the Muslim World which is also expressed in the business accepted by the banks and in the way they operate.

3. Hypothesis: There is common ethical ground of Muslims and Christians in some parts of the banking sector in that the business accepted by the banks and the way they operate is at least partially the same.

4. Hypothesis: There is potential for co-operation between Muslims and Christians, because their business and the way they operate would allow to work together for the benefit of both.

67

B. Returns

With 34 banks out of 119 answering the questionnaire sent out to them, a good number of returns was achieved. The number of returns is very satisfactory, because the study had to cope with geographical distances, cultural and linguistic barriers.

Within the group of co-operative banks, the ratio was higher with 14 out of 35, and lower within the group of Islamic banks with only 21 out of 91.

- These difference might be partly due to the fact that within the first group, 23 companies were based in the country out of which the study was conducted and people might tend to answer rather to a "national" study than to a request from outside the country.

- Also, the 9 banks in Iran and the 5 banks in Sudan out of which not a single one answered were all part of group two. In the case of these two countries it was difficult to obtain support from the countries' embassies.

For practical reasons, a number of questionnaires was sent by fax, other copies were distributed by letter. Most questionnaires were sent directly to the banks under review, whereas others were sent to them via the countries' embassies. There were also some combinations of these ways of contacting the financial institutions. No relation was observed between the type of contact used and the return ratio.

Most banks reacted within less than a month. Over time, returns continued however. Answers were registered even five months after the sending out of faxes.

C. Islamic banking

In this part, the findings on Islamic banks are presented and analysed. The banks included in this section will be presented in two groups: the first group consists of Islamic banks in Europe, the second one out of their counterparts in the Muslim World. It has to be noted that the institutions are classified according to their administrative (head-) office. This means, that the Dar Al-Maal Al-Islami (DMI) Trust is listed as an example for Islamic banking in Europe, although it also has numerous activities in the Muslim World, or that ABC International Bank plc is listed with banks in the Muslim World because the group's headquarters are in that area, even if ABC International Bank plc itself is established in Europe.

Among the banks in the Muslim world, a number of sub-groups can be differentiated:

- First, the Islamic Development Bank will be presented as a *supra-national government bank*.

- The following two groups represent banks which form *trusts involved in Islamic Banking* such as the Albaraka Investment and Development Company and the Arab Banking Corporation.

- In a fourth group, *local Islamic banks* like Faisal Islamic Bank of Egypt S.A. or Bank Islam Malaysia Berhad are summarised.

- A fifth group was formed by banks of Pakistan as *the case of Pakistan*.

Translation of Arabic terms are provided throughout the text. An overview of Arabic terms is provided in the appendices on page 131.

1. Islamic banking in Europe

Dar Al-Maal Al-Islami (DMI) Trust

(1) DMI headquarters and administration

(a) General presentation of the institution

Dar Al-Maal Al-Islami (DMI) Trust[84] was established in the Commonwealth of the Bahamas in July 1981, while the trust administrator was established in Switzerland. Reasons for this configuration include tax issues. DMI was based on the experiences gained with the Faisal Islamic Bank of Egypt S.A. and was founded in order to establish a link between Europe and the Muslim world and to support the establishment of further Islamic banks in other countries.

The latter is analysed in the chapter "Local Islamic banks", because there are no plans for it to be integrated into the DMI structure. However, it is important in that it was founded before DMI and served as a pilot.

There is an external supervisory body for Dar Al-Maal Al-Islami (DMI) Trust.

Today, the Dar Al-Maal Al-Islami (DMI) Trust has activities mainly in Europe, but also in areas including the Near and Middle East, Africa, the Indian Subcontinent and Southeast Asia. A more detailed overview is provided in the following table on page 71.

In addition, the group runs its own consultancy company, the Pan Islamic Consultancy Services Istishara S.A. The Massraf Faysal Al-Islami Ltd bank is dormant and has been for the last several years.

Faisal Finance (Switzerland) S.A., the Pan Islamic Consultancy Services Istishara S.A., the Islamic Investment Company of the Gulf (Bahrain) E.C. and the Islamic Takafol and Retakafol (Bahamas) Company Ltd will be analysed in separate sections in the following.

---

[84] In Arab, *dar* means "gate" and *maal* means "property".

70

Europe

Denmark

- Faisal Finance (Denmark) A/S

Jersey

- The Islamic Investment Company Ltd
- Massraf Faysal Al-Islami (Jersey) Ltd
- DMI Administrative Services Ltd

Luxembourg

- Takafol S.A.
- Faisal Finance (Luxembourg) S.A.

Netherlands

- Faisal Finance (Netherlands) BV

Switzerland

- Faisal Finance (Switzerland) S.A.
- Pan Islamic Consultancy Services Istishara S.A.

United Kingdom

- Takafol (U.K.) Ltd

Africa

Egypt

- Islamic Investment and Development Company

Guinea

- Banque Islamique de Guinée

Niger

- Banque Islamique du Niger

Senegal

- Banque Islamique du Sénégal

Indian Subcontinent

Pakistan

- Faysal Bank Ltd
- Al-Faysal Investment Bank Ltd

Southeast Asia

Indonesia

- DMI Trust Representative Office

Near and Middle East

Bahrain

- Islamic Investment Company of the Gulf (Bahrain) E.C.
- Faysal Islamic Bank of Bahrain E.C.
- Takafol Islamic Insurance Company, Bahrain E.C.
- Faysal Investment Bank of Bahrain E.C.

Qatar

- Islamic Investment Company of the Gulf (Sharjah)

Saudi Arabia

- Islamic Investment Company of the Gulf (Sharjah)
- Faysal Islamic Bank of Bahrain E.C.
- Faisal Finance (Switzerland) S.A.
- Takafol Islamic Insurance Company, Bahrain E.C.
- Islamic Takafol and Retakafol (Bahamas) Company Ltd

Turkey

- Faisal Finance Institution Inc.

United Arab Emirates

- Islamic Investment Company of the Gulf (Sharjah)

Other

Bahamas

- Islamic Investment Company of the Gulf (Bahamas) Ltd
- Massraf Faysal Al-Islami Ltd
- Islamic Takafol and Retakafol (Bahamas) Company Ltd
- Istishara Consulting Trust, Bahamas

Netherlands Antilles

- Faisal Finance (Netherlandse Antilles) NV

Table 1. Activities of
Dar Al-Maal Al-Islami (DMI) Trust

There are holders of approximately 14,000 to 15,000 equity participation certificates.

Directors include the founder, Prince Mohammed Al-Faisal Al-Saoud (chairman; also chairman of the executive committee), Mr. Muazzam Ali (vice chairman) and Mr. Aminu Dantata (vice chairman).

Chairman of the management committee is Omar Abdi Ali.

There is a religious supervisory board, i.e. a shariah supervisory council. Its chairman is His Eminence Mohamed Khater Mohamed Al-Sheikh.

(b) Objectives of the institution and services offered by the institution

The Dar Al-Maal Al-Islami (DMI) Trust's general objectives are to offer contemporary Islamic financial services, to do its business in compliance with the rules of Shariah, to promote the Islamic economic and financial system by implementing its various activities through subsidiaries inside and outside the Muslim World, and to support development programs by promoting the co-operation within the Muslim community.

Dar Al-Maal Al-Islami (DMI) Trust is active in private banking, provides current and saving accounts, deposit accounts, i.e. long and short term investment accounts, commercial loans, letters of credit and guarantee and foreign exchange services.

The trust is also involved in participation financing leading to acquisition or *ijara-wa-iktina*, leasing or *ijara*, manufacturing financing or *istisna*, advance payment sale or *salam*, sale and resale financing or *morabaha* and interest-free loans or *qard hassan*.

Dar Al-Maal Al-Islami (DMI) Trust considers that investment in conventional national and international equities is permitted, with certain restrictions. The trust is active in participation financing or *modaraba*, as well as in mutual participation financing or *musharaka*.

(c) Specifically religious business attitudes

Daily prayer times are practised. The period of fasting is kept. The client base is mixed; there are Muslims as well as non-Muslims.

72

(d) Future Outlook

There are new products being planned. Implementations in other locations and markets are also being planned. At the same time, DMI wants to consolidate its position.

(2) Faisal Finance (Switzerland) S.A.

(a) General presentation of the institution

Faisal Finance (Switzerland) S.A. was established in Switzerland in 1990.

Today, the Faisal Finance (Switzerland) S.A. has one office in Geneva.

The breakdown of shareholders and their respective parts is as follows: The founder, Dar Al-Maal Al-Islami (DMI) Trust, owns 100 % of the shares.

There is a religious supervisory board, i.e. the shariah supervisory council of DMI.

(b) Objectives of the institution and services offered by the institution

Faisal Finance (Switzerland) S.A.'s general objectives are to offer contemporary Islamic financial services, to do its business in compliance with the rules of Shariah and to promote the Islamic economic and financial system.

Faisal Finance (Switzerland) S.A. is active in private banking, deposit accounts, commercial loans, letters of credit and guarantee and foreign exchange services.

The institution is also involved in leasing or *ijara* and manufacturing financing or *istisna*. Faisal Finance (Switzerland) S.A. is also active in participation financing or *modaraba*

(c) Specifically religious business attitudes

Daily prayer times are practised. There are no particularities during the period of fasting. The client base of 1,300 clients is total Muslim.

(d) Future Outlook

There are there new products being planned, i. e. Islamic funds. It is also planned to open an office in Saudi Arabia.

(3) Pan Islamic Consultancy Services Istishara S.A.

(a) General presentation of the institution

The Pan Islamic Consultancy Services Istishara S.A. was established in Switzerland in 1984.

Today, the Pan Islamic Consultancy Services Istishara S.A. has two offices in two locations, i.e. Geneva and Cairo.

The company is part of the Dar Al-Maal Al-Islami (DMI) Trust.

Pan Islamic Consultancy Services Istishara S.A. keeps information on founder members or directors confidential.

There is a religious supervisory board, i.e. a shariah supervisory council.

(b) Objectives of the institution and services offered by the institution

Pan Islamic Consultancy Services Istishara S.A.'s general objectives are to provide management consultancy, to offer contemporary Islamic financial services, to do its business in compliance with the rules of Shariah, to promote the Islamic economic and financial system and to fund development programs.

(c) Specifically religious business attitudes

Daily prayer times are practised. The period of fasting is kept. The company is closed on Muslim holidays

(4) Islamic Investment Company of the Gulf (Bahrain) E.C.

(a) General presentation of the institution

The Islamic Investment Company of the Gulf (Bahrain) E.C. was established in Bahrain in January 1983. According to the institution, the rules of general Islamic Shariah Law are incorporated in the state's law.

There is an external supervisory body for Islamic Investment Company of the Gulf (Bahrain) E.C., namely the Bahrain Monetary Agency, which is the central bank.

74

Today, the Islamic Investment Company of the Gulf (Bahrain) E.C. has one office in Bahrain.

The Dar Al Maal Al Islami Trust owns 100 % of the shares.

Directors are H.R.H. Prince Mohamed Al Faisal Al Saud, Dr. Abdulaziz Abdulla Alfadda, Sh. Haider M. Binladen, Mr. Omar A. Ali and Dr. Mahmoud El Helw.

There is a religious supervisory board, i.e. a shariah supervisory council.

(b) Objectives of the institution and services offered by the institution

The Islamic Investment Company of the Gulf (Bahrain) E.C.'s general objective according to the mission statement is to be a premier Islamic Investment Bank, providing value-added products and services to the customers in line with the rules of Shariah in order to optimise shareholder value through an organisational culture based on learning and fairness. It wants to promote the Islamic economic and financial system, to fund development programs and believes in creativity in all fields of activity. Shared values are *iitihad* (referendum), *iima* (consensus) and *ouavas* (proactive thinking).

The Islamic Investment Company of the Gulf (Bahrain) E.C. is active in private banking, provides current and saving accounts, as well as deposit accounts, i.e. based on the modaraba concept, monthly, quarterly, 6 monthly and yearly.

The Islamic Investment Company of the Gulf (Bahrain) E.C. is also involved in participation financing leading to acquisition or *ijara-wa-iktina*, leasing or *ijara*, manufacturing financing or *istisna*, advance payment sale or *salam*, sale and resale financing or *morabaha* and interest-free loans or *qard hassan*.

The Islamic Investment Company of the Gulf (Bahrain) E.C. considers that investment in conventional national and international equities is permitted, in compliance with the Sharia ethics. The Islamic Investment Company of the Gulf (Bahrain) E.C. is active in participation financing or *modaraba*, both restricted and unrestricted, as well as in mutual participation financing or *musharaka*. The institution is also involved in *istisna*, m & a, equities and corporate finance.

(c) Specifically religious business attitudes

Daily prayer times are practised. The period of fasting is kept. The bank invites Islamic scholars to discuss different issues related to Islam and practices daily five or ten minute recitations on different subjects, i.e. jurisprudence, *hadith* or *thafsir*. In addition, offsight lectures and classes on Islam are attended.

The client base is mixed; there are Muslims as well as non-Muslims.

(d) Future Outlook

There are new products being planned, i. e. in different areas related to corporate finance, capital markets and structured finance. Implementations in other locations and markets are planned in OECD countries and in the regions Asia Pacific and South East Asia. Priority is given to countries of the Organisation of Islamic Conference OIC.

(5) Islamic Takafol and Retakafol (Bahamas) Company Ltd

(a) General presentation of the institution

The Islamic Takafol and Retakafol (Bahamas) Company Ltd was established on the Bahamas in October 1983. Similarly to the establishment of DMI trust, reasons why the company was based on the Bahamas included tax issues. According to the institution, the rules of Takafol are incorporated in the state's law.

There is an external supervisory body for Islamic Takafol and Retakafol (Bahamas) Company Ltd.

Today, the Islamic Takafol and Retakafol (Bahamas) Company Ltd has two offices in two locations, i.e. Nassau and Jeddah.

The breakdown of shareholders and their respective parts is as follows:

Dar Al-Maal Al-Islami (DMI) Trust	99,995 shares
H.E. Dr. Omar Abdel Rahman Azzam	1 share
H.E. Sheikh Abdallah Ahmed Zainal Alireza	1 share
Mr. Omar Abdi Ali	2 shares
Dr. Moustafa Hosny	1 share

Table 2. Breakdown of shareholders of
Islamic Takafol and Retakafol (Bahamas) Company

The Dar Al-Maal Al-Islami (DMI) Trust has founded the company.

Directors are H.E. Mr. Abdel Kader Koshak, H.E. Sheikh Abdallah Ahmed Zainal Alireza, H.E. Dr. Abdelaziz Abdallah Alfadda and Mr. Omar Abdi Ali.

There is a religious supervisory board, i.e. a shariah supervisory council, which is that of DMI.

(b) Objectives of the institution and services offered by the institution

Islamic Takafol and Retakafol (Bahamas) Company Ltd's general objectives are to administer Islamically approved insurance and re-insurance services, to do its business in compliance with the rules of Shariah, to promote the Islamic economic and financial system and to fund development programs.

The institution is involved in takafol, i. e. solidarity near the conventional insurance and reinsurance.

Islamic Takafol and Retakafol (Bahamas) Company Ltd is also involved in interest-free loans or *qard hassan*.

(c) Specifically religious business attitudes

There were no such attitudes reported. There are no particularities during the period of fasting. The client base is total Muslim.

(d) Future Outlook

For the time being, there are no new products being planned. Implementations in other locations and markets may follow. The priority is to consolidate the present situation.

2. Islamic banking in the Muslim World

a) Supra-national government banks

In this group of institutions, the most important one is the Islamic Development Bank, because it was one of the first of its type and is by far the biggest.

Islamic Development Bank

(a) General presentation of the institution

The Islamic Development Bank was established in Saudi Arabia in July 1975 by means of a treaty between 29 governments. It is an OPEC aid institution, which means that it receives its funds from the Organization of the Petroleum Exporting Countries.

Today, the Islamic Development Bank has its principal office in Saudi Arabia and two regional offices in Morocco and Malaysia.

The breakdown of shareholders and their respective parts is given in the following table. All amounts are in millions of Islamic Dinars. Founder members are marked by an asterix (*). The first amount corresponds to the initial subscriptions before October 1974, the second to the subscriptions as of August 1995.

Founder		Country	Oct 74	Aug 95
*	1.	The Afghanistan Republic	2.5	5.0
	2.	Albania		2.5
*	3.	Algerian Democratic and Popular Republic	25.0	124.3
	4.	Azerbaijan		4.9
*	5.	State of Bahrain	5.0	7.0
*	6.	Republic of Bangladesh	10.0	49.3
	7.	Benin		4.9
	8.	Brunei Darussalam		12.4
	9.	Burkina Faso		12.4
	10.	Cameroon		12.4
*	11.	Republic of Chad	2.5	4.9
	12.	Comoros		2.5
	13.	Djibouti		2.5
*	14.	Arab Republic of Egypt	25.0	49.3
	15.	Gabon		14.8
	16.	Gambia		2.5
*	17.	Republic Guinea	2.5	12.4
	18.	Guinea-Bissau		2.5
*	19.	Republic of Indonesia	25.0	124.3
	20.	Iran		350.0
	21.	Iraq		13.1
*	22.	Hashemite Kingdom of Jordan	4.0	19.9
*	23.	State of Kuwait	100.0	496.7
	24.	Kyrghyzstan		2.5
*	25.	Republic of Lebanon	2.5	4.9
*	26.	Arab Republic of Libya	125.0	400.0
*	27.	Malaysia	16.0	79.6
	28.	Maldives		2.5
*	29.	Republic of Mali	2.5	4.9
*	30.	Islamic Republic of Mauritania	2.5	4.9
*	31.	Kingdom of Morocco	5.0	24.8
*	32.	Republic of Niger	2.5	12.4
*	33.	Sultanate of Oman	5.0	13.8
*	34.	Islamic Republic of Pakistan	25.0	124.3
	35.	Palestine		9.9
*	36.	State of Qatar	25.0	49.3
*	37.	Kingdom of Saudi Arabia	200.0	997.2
*	38.	Republic of Senegal	2.5	12.4
	39.	Sierra Leone		2.5
*	40.	Democratic Republic of Somalia	2.5	2.5
*	41.	Democratic Republic of Sudan	10.0	19.7
*	42.	The Syrian Arab Republic	2.5	5.0
*	43.	Republic of Tunisia	2.5	9.9
*	44.	Republic of Turkey	10.0	315.5
	45.	Turkmenistan		2.5
	46.	Uganda		12.4
*	47.	State of United Arab Emirates	110.0	283.1
*	48.	The Yemen Arab Republic	2.5	24.8
		TOTAL	755.0	3751.8

Table 3. Breakdown of member country subscriptions of
Islamic Development Bank 1974 and 1995

The Board of Governors consists of two representatives from each member country, who are of ministerial status in most cases. The Board of Governors elects the President of the Bank. The Board of Executive Directors is composed of eleven members, five of whom are appointed by the five largest subscriber countries (at present: Kingdom of Saudi Arabia, State of Kuwait, Arab Republic of Libya, Iran and Republic of Turkey) and six are elected by the other member countries. There is no religious supervisory board, i.e. no shariah supervisory council.

(b) Objectives of the institution and services offered by the institution

The Islamic Development Bank's general objective according to the articles of agreement is to foster economic development and social progress of member countries and Muslim communities individually as well as jointly in accordance with the principles of the Shariah. It wants to promote the Islamic economic and financial system and to fund development programs.

The Islamic Development Bank is involved in leasing or *ijara*, sale and resale financing or *morabaha* and interest-free loans or *qard hassan*. The bank is active in participation financing or *modaraba*, as well as in mutual participation financing or *musharaka*. The institution is also involved in project financing, technical assistance, import trade financing, longer-term trade financing and special assistance operations.

(c) Specifically religious business attitudes

The Islamic Development Bank has for a long time been the largest OPEC aid institution. In 1993, the bank was nearly double the size of the next-biggest OPEC aid institution:

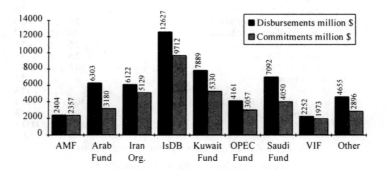

Illustration 11. OPEC aid institutions in 1993

80

(d) Future Outlook

The priorities for the bank's future are the integration of new members, development through co-operation, enhancement of human resources, poverty alleviation and care for the environment.

b) Albaraka Investment and Development Company

Albaraka Islamic Investment Bank

(a) General presentation of the institution

The Albaraka Islamic Investment Bank was established in Bahrain in 1984.

There is an external supervisory body for Albaraka Islamic Investment Bank, namely the Bahrain Monetary Agency, which is the central bank.

Today, the Albaraka Islamic Investment Bank has four offices in two countries, i.e. Bahrain and Pakistan. It is at the core of the Albaraka Investment and Development Company, which consists of 231 companies including fifteen banks with a total of 60 branches and is located in thirty-three countries with activities in forty-three countries.

The breakdown of shareholders and their respective parts is as follows: apart from many individuals, the Albaraka Investment and Development Company, Jeddah, owns 51 % of the shares.

Albaraka was established by Sheikh Saleh Abdullah Kamel who holds 50 % of the capital.

He is also chairman of the Board of Directors; deputy chairman is Mahmoud Jameel Hassoubah.

General manager is Abdullah Abolfatih Ali.

There is a religious supervisory board, i.e. a *shariah* supervisory council.

(b) Objectives of the institution and services offered by the institution

Albaraka Islamic Investment Bank's general objectives are to offer contemporary Islamic financial services, to do its business in compliance with the rules of Shariah and to promote the Islamic economic and financial system.

81

The bank is active in private banking, provides current and saving accounts, deposit accounts, i.e. joint and specific, letters of credit and guarantee and foreign exchange services.

Albaraka Islamic Investment Bank is also involved in participation financing leading to acquisition or *ijara-wa-iktina*, leasing or *ijara*, manufacturing financing or *istisna*, advance payment sale or *salam* and interest-free loans or *qard hassan*.

Albaraka Islamic Investment Bank is active in participation financing or *modaraba*, both restricted and unrestricted, as well as in mutual participation financing or *musharaka*. The institution is also involved in other financial services.

(c) Specifically religious business attitudes

Daily prayer times are practised. The period of fasting is kept.

(d) Future Outlook

There are new products being planned. Implementations in other locations and markets are also being planned. Priority is given to real estate investment funds.

c) Arab Banking Corporation

(1) Bahrain Islamic Bank

(a) General presentation of the institution

The Bahrain Islamic Bank was established in Bahrain in February 1979. According to the institution, all Islamic Principles are incorporated in the state's law.

There is an external supervisory body for Bahrain Islamic Bank, namely the Bahrain Monetary Agency, which is the central bank.

Today, the Bahrain Islamic Bank has five offices in Bahrain.

The Arab Banking Corporation (B.S.C.) owns 100 % of the shares.

Founder is Mr. Abdul Latif Janahi.

There is a religious supervisory board, i.e. a shariah supervisory council.

82

(b) Objectives of the institution and services offered by the institution

Bahrain Islamic Bank's general objectives are to offer contemporary Islamic financial services, to do its business in compliance with the rules of Shariah and to promote the Islamic economic and financial system.

Bahrain Islamic Bank provides current and saving accounts, deposit accounts, commercial loans, letters of credit and guarantee and foreign exchange services.

Bahrain Islamic Bank is also involved in participation financing leading to acquisition or *ijara-wa-iktina*, leasing or *ijara*, advance payment sale or *salam*, sale and resale financing or *morabaha* and interest-free loans or *qard hassan*.

Bahrain Islamic Bank is active in participation financing or *modaraba*, as well as in mutual participation financing or *musharaka*.

(c) Specifically religious business attitudes

Daily prayer times are practised. The period of fasting is kept. The client base is total Muslim.

(d) Future Outlook

There are new products being planned. Implementations in other locations and markets are also being planned.

(2) ABC International Bank plc

(a) General presentation of the institution

The ABC International Bank plc was established in UK in 1991. There is an external supervisory body for ABC International Bank plc, namely the Bank of England.

Today, the ABC International Bank plc has three offices in London (2) and in Paris (1). The Arab Banking Corporation (B.S.C.) owns 100 % of the shares.

The chairman of the board of directors is Sheikh Khalid Ali Alturki; the deputy chairman and executive director is Mr. Stanislas M. Yassukovish.

There is a religious supervisory board, i.e. a shariah supervisory council, at parent level.

(b) Objectives of the institution and services offered by the institution

ABC International Bank plc's general objective according to the mission statement is to increase the ABC Group's share of financing Euro-Arab trade. It also wants to offer contemporary Islamic financial services and to do its business in compliance with the rules of Shariah.

ABC International Bank plc is active in private banking, provides current and saving accounts, deposit accounts, commercial loans, letters of credit and guarantee and foreign exchange services.

ABC International Bank plc is also involved in manufacturing financing or *istisna*, and sale and resale financing or *morabaha*.

(c) Specifically religious business attitudes

There were no such attitudes reported. There are no particularities during the period of fasting.

(d) Future Outlook

There are new products being planned. Implementations in other locations and markets are also being planned. The priorities is the development of trade/project finance opportunities; ABC International Bank plc is actively looking at various Islamically-structured facilities. The main activity is however located at the parent in Bahrain.

d) Local Islamic banks

(1) Faisal Islamic Bank of Egypt S.A.

(a) General presentation of the institution

Faisal Islamic Bank of Egypt S.A. was established in Egypt in August 1977. According to the institution, sharia banking rules are incorporated in the state's law. On 3 October 1977, the Ministry of Waqf issued a Ministerial Decree enacting the status of the bank and on 5 July 1979, the bank was officially inaugurated.

Today, the Faisal Islamic Bank of Egypt S.A. has one headoffice and 14 branches in different zones of Egypt, i.e. the Cairo, Alexandria, Canal and Upper Egypt zone.

Founder is Prince Mohammed Al-Faisal Al-Saoud. He is still chairman of the board today.

There is a religious supervisory board, i.e. a shariah supervisory council.

(b) Objectives of the institution and services offered by the institution

Faisal Islamic Bank of Egypt S.A.'s general objectives are to offer contemporary Islamic financial services, to do its business in compliance with the rules of Shariah, to promote the Islamic economic and financial system and to fund development programs.

The bank is active in private banking, provides current and saving accounts, deposit accounts and commercial loans.

Faisal Islamic Bank of Egypt S.A. is also involved in advance payment sale or salam, sale and resale financing or *morabaha* and interest-free loans or *qard hassan*.

Faisal Islamic Bank of Egypt S.A. is active in participation financing or *modaraba*, as well as in mutual participation financing or *musharaka*.

(c) Specifically religious business attitudes

Daily prayer times are practised. No particularities during the period of fasting were reported. The client base is almost 100 % Muslim.

(2) Faisal Islamic Bank of Kibris Limited

(a) General presentation of the institution

The Faisal Islamic Bank of Kibris Limited was established in Turkey in October 1982. According to the institution, sharia banking rules are incorporated in the state's law.

There is an external supervisory body for Faisal Islamic Bank of Kibris Limited, namely the Central Bank of The Turkish Republic of Northern Cyprus.

Today, the Faisal Islamic Bank of Kibris Limited has four offices in four countries.

The breakdown of shareholders and their respective parts is as follows: Kooheji family 72.01 %, Dubai Islamic Bank 19.62 %, Al Gosaibi Investment Holding E.C. 3.31%.

Founders are members of the Kooheji family from Bahrain.

Directors include Abdulla Abduljabbar Kooheji, Chairman and Managing Director, Ahmet M.O.H. Alshamsi (Dubai Islamic Bank) Maan Al Sanea (Al Gosaibi Investment Holding E.C.) and Mehmet Barut (Secretary).

Management and board members are Abdulla Abduljabbar Kooheji, Chairman and Managing Director, Jamal S. Gheith, Operations Manager, Kaukab Jamal Zuberi, Marketing Manager, Cemile Senkalp, Finance Manager and Altay Haydar, Administrative Manager.

There is a religious supervisory board, i.e. a shariah supervisory council, which consist of Sheikh Dr. Abdullatif El-Mahmoud, Sheikh Nizam Yaqubi and Sheikh Abdulmannan Othman.

(b) Objectives of the institution and services offered by the institution

Faisal Islamic Bank of Kibris Limited's general objectives are to offer contemporary Islamic financial services, to do its business in compliance with the rules of Shariah, to promote the Islamic economic and financial system and to provide planned strategies for restructuring.

Faisal Islamic Bank of Kibris Limited is active in private banking, provides current and saving accounts, deposit accounts, i.e. term deposits of personal and corporate bodies, commercial loans, letters of credit and guarantee and foreign exchange services.

Faisal Islamic Bank of Kibris Limited is also involved in participation financing leading to acquisition or *ijara-wa-iktina*, sale and resale financing or *morabaha* and interest-free loans or *qard hassan*.

Faisal Islamic Bank of Kibris Limited considers that investment in conventional national and international equities is allowed. Faisal Islamic Bank of Kibris Limited is active in participation financing or *modaraba*, but in unrestricted only, as well as in mutual participation financing or *musharaka*.

(c) Specifically religious business attitudes

The period of fasting is kept. The bank has a *zakat* fund which receives the bank's *zakat* and other contributions from individuals and spends it in its Sharia channels under the supervision of the religious supervisory board.

86

According to the bank, the client base is made up of approximately 1,000 Muslims dwelling either in The Turkish Republic of Northern Cyprus or other Muslim countries. Is should be pointed out that The Turkish Republic of Northern Cyprus is only recognised by Turkey.

(3) Malayan Banking Berhad

(a) General presentation of the institution

The Malayan Banking Berhad was established in Malaysia in 1960. It sees itself as the leader of the Malaysian banking industry for nearly four decades and major contributor to Malaysia's ascent to international recognition. According to the institution, all Islamic Principles are incorporated in the state's law.

There is an external supervisory body for Malayan Banking Berhad, namely the Central bank.

Today, the Malayan Banking Berhad has 230 offices in 11 countries.

The breakdown of the major shareholders and their respective parts is as follows:

Pemegang Amanah Raya M'sia Skim ASB	553,895,500 shares	48.44 %
HSBC (Kuala Lumpur) Nominees Sdn Bhd	112,612,720 shares	9.85 %
Cartaban (Malaya) Nominees Sdn Bhd	90,669,124 shares	7.95 %

Table 4. Breakdown of the major shareholders of
Malayan Banking Berhad

The current paid-up capital of the bank is RM 1,143,413,707, corresponding to 1,143,413,707 shares. More than 95 % of the issued capital is held by shareholders who hold more than 1,000,000 shares.

Founders are members of the Khoo's family.

The board of directors includes Dato' Mohamed Basir bin Ahmad (chairman), Dato' Richard Ho Ung Hun (vice chairman), Amirsham A Aziz (managing director) and Mohd Salleh bin Hj. Harun (executive director).

(b) Objectives of the institution and services offered by the institution

Malayan Banking Berhad's general objectives are to offer contemporary Islamic financial services with its interest-free banking department, to do its business in compliance with the rules of Shariah, to promote the Islamic economic and financial system and to fund development programs.

Malayan Banking Berhad is active in private banking, provides current and saving accounts, deposit accounts, commercial loans, letters of credit and guarantee and foreign exchange services.

Malayan Banking Berhad is also involved in participation financing leading to acquisition or *ijara-wa-iktina*, sale and resale financing or *morabaha* and interest-free loans or *qard hassan*.

Malayan Banking Berhad is active in participation financing or *modaraba*, as well as in mutual participation financing or *musharaka*.

(c) Specifically religious business attitudes

Daily prayer times are practised. There are no particularities during the period of fasting.

(d) Future Outlook

There are new products being planned. Implementations in other locations and markets are also being planned, but no priorities are fixed.

(4) Bank Islam Malaysia Berhad

(a) General presentation of the institution

The Bank Islam Malaysia Berhad was established in Malaysia in March 1983.

The establishment of the bank as the first Islamic bank in Malaysia was preceded by long-lasting preparations, following the establishment of the Islamic Development Bank. They culminated in a report of a "National Steering Committee on Islamic Bank" which was prepared under the guidance of the Prime Minister of Malaysia. Following the acceptance of the report by the government, the parliament and senate legislated the Islamic Banking Act in 1982.

Today, the Bank Islam Malaysia Berhad has 79 offices in Malaysia.

The breakdown of the major shareholders and their respective parts is as follows:

Pilgrims' Management and Fund Board	26.76 %
Albaraka Investment & Development Company	9.88 %
Majilis Ugama Islam Sabah	5.94 %
Lembaga Tabung Angkatan Tentera	4.95 %
Jami Company Sendirian Berhad	3.95 %
Muslim Welfare Organisation of Malaysia	3.22 %
Majilis Ugama Islam Selangor	3.08 %
Majilis Amanah Rakyat	2.97 %
Perbadanan Pemasaran	2.97 %
Amin Baitul Mal Johor	2.97 %

Table 5. Breakdown of the major shareholders of
Bank Islam Malaysia Berhad

The current paid-up capital of the bank is RM 133.405 million. The Minister of Finance holds one Special Rights Redeemable Preference Share of RM 1.

Chairman of the board of directors is YBhg. Tan Sri Dato' Shamsuddin Abdul Kadir; managing director is Encik Ahmad Tajudin bin Abdul Rahman.

There is a religious supervisory board, i.e. a shariah supervisory council. The bank's articles of association provide:

"... A Religious Supervisory Council, whose members would be made up of Muslim religious scholars in the country, shall be established to advise the company on the operations of its banking business. ..."

"... The Religious Supervisory Council shall have a minimum of three and a maximum of seven members whose appointment shall be acceptable to the Minister for a term not exceeding two years and each member is eligible for reappointment. ..."

(b) Objectives of the institution and services offered by the institution

Bank Islam Malaysia Berhad's general objectives are to offer contemporary Islamic financial services, to do its business in compliance with the rules of Shariah, to promote the Islamic economic and financial system, and to fund development programs.

The bank is active in private banking, provides current and saving accounts, deposit accounts, letters of credit and guarantee and foreign exchange services.

Bank Islam Malaysia Berhad is also involved in leasing or *ijara*, manufacturing financing or *istisna*, sale and resale financing or *morabaha* and interest-free loans or *qard hassan*.

The institution considers that investment in conventional national and international equities is not permitted. Bank Islam Malaysia Berhad is active in participation financing or *modaraba*, both restricted and unrestricted.

(c) Specifically religious business attitudes

Daily prayer times are practised. There are no particularities during the period of fasting.

The client base is made up of 489,469 people. No record is kept of religious affiliations.

(d) Future Outlook

There are new products being planned. Implementations in other locations and markets are also being planned, but no priorities are fixed.

(5) Bank Muamalat

(a) General presentation of the institution

The Bank Muamalat was established in Indonesia in May 1992. The establishment of the bank was preceded by a workshop on "Bank Interest and Banking" and a work group under the guidance of Mr. Prodjo Kusumo. Their plan to set up a non-interest bank was strengthened by several members of the former and current government. According to the institution, Sharia Banking are incorporated in the state's law.

Today, the Bank Muamalat has one head office, three branch offices, four sub-branch offices and 11 cash offices in Indonesia.

Founder members are 227 individuals, mostly Islamic entrepreneurs.

Directors are Drs. Haji Zainulbahar Noor (president director), Haji Maman Wirasa Natapermadi, Haji Drs. Atang M. Saptari and Haji Drs. Ismail A. Said. There is a board of commissioners with five members.

There is a religious supervisory board, i.e. a shariah supervisory council. Its chairman is Mr. Kyai Haji Hasan Basri.

(b) Objectives of the institution and services offered by the institution

Bank Muamalat's general objectives according to the mission statement are to assist in the development of the nation's economy, primarily by enhancing the role of the Muslim people and entrepreneurs and maximising its economic value to its shareholders, while addressing its social responsibilities. It wants to offer contemporary Islamic financial services, to do its business in compliance with the rules of Shariah, to fund development programs and to improve the quality of the people's socio-economic life in order to narrow the socio-economic gap and to promote the participation of the people in the process of development especially in the financial area.

The bank provides current and saving accounts, deposit accounts, commercial loans, letters of credit and guarantee and foreign exchange services.

Bank Muamalat is also involved in sale and resale financing or *morabaha* and interest-free loans or *qard hassan*.

The bank is active in participation financing or *modaraba*.

(c) Specifically religious business attitudes

There were no such attitudes reported. There are no particularities during the period of fasting. However, the client base is almost 100 % Muslim.

e) The case of Pakistan

Pakistan has tried to establish Islamic principles as a standard in banking since it became an independent state. Only in recent years, these attempts have been converted in practical legislation on banking. Today, a non-interest based Islamic banking system is incorporated in the state's law. The State Bank of Pakistan plays a major role in the process of Islamisation, because it controls the financial sector via rulings. Pakistan could be seen as a sample country for other countries in which Islam has strong political support.

(1) Muslim Commercial Bank

(a) General presentation of the institution

The Muslim Commercial Bank was established in Pakistan in July 1947. There is an external supervisory body for the bank.

Today, the Muslim Commercial Bank has 1321 offices in Pakistan, Sri Lanka, Bangladesh and Bahrain. The breakdown of shareholders and their respective parts is as follows:

Federal Government	6.698 %
State Bank of Pakistan	14.901 %
Joint Stock Companies	39.393 %
Individuals	26.662 %
Insurance Companies	3.300 %
Financial Institutions	1.757 %
Foreign Companies	6.791 %
Leasing Companies	0.092 %
Modaraba Companies	0.375 %
Investment Companies	0.029 %
Others	0.002 %
Total	100.000 %

Table 6. Breakdown of shareholders of
Muslim Commercial Bank

Founder members are Sir Adamjee Haji Dawood and Mr. M.A.H. Ispahani. President and Chief Executive of the board of directors is Mr. Husain Lawai.

There are religious supervisory boards, i.e. the Islamic Banking Division in the bank and the Islamic Advisory council in the country.

(b) Objectives of the institution and services offered by the institution

Muslim Commercial Bank's general objectives are to offer contemporary Islamic financial services, to do its business in compliance with the rules of Shariah, to promote the Islamic economic and financial system, and to fund development programs.

Muslim Commercial Bank provides current and saving accounts, deposit accounts, commercial loans, letters of credit and guarantee and foreign exchange services.

Muslim Commercial Bank is also involved in participation financing leading to acquisition or *ijara-wa-iktina*, leasing or *ijara*, sale and resale financing or *morabaha* and interest-free loans or *qard hassan*.

The bank is active in mutual participation financing or *musharaka*.

(c) Specifically religious business attitudes

Daily prayer times are practised. The period of fasting is kept. Haji is respected.

The client base is made up of 4.128 million people; no distinction is made on the basis of religion.

(d) Future Outlook

There are new products and the implementation in other locations and markets being planned, including:

- A leasing company, the International Leasing & Financial Services Limited, incorporated in Dhaka, Bangladesh, in partnership with one multinational company and one insurance company of Bangladesh,

- A joint venture bank which will be a subsidiary of the Muslim Commercial Bank named Mercantile Commercial Bank Limited in Tanzania,

- Incorporating finance companies in London and in Hong Kong and opening of overseas branches of Muslim Commercial Bank, one in Romania, one in Sharjah, and two in Sri Lanka,

- Extension of an on-line banking network to include 200 branches,

- Installation of automatic transfer machines at 100 branches all over the country,

- Installation of a Voice Response System, so that customers can obtain the balance in their account and order cheque books by telephone and arrangement for customers to get their bank statement on fax.

(2) Agricultural Development Bank of Pakistan

(a) General presentation of the institution

The Agricultural Development Bank of Pakistan was established in Pakistan in February 1961.

The bank, which is the largest developing financing institution, used to be a so called big landowner's bank. In 1995, an important development in the bank's history took place with the transformation to a small farmers bank: Loans to landless and small farmers are

93

provided at the doorstep of the customers, tractors for rural people are financed and credit is increasingly given to women.

There is an external supervisory body for Agricultural Development Bank of Pakistan, namely the State Bank of Pakistan and the Government of Pakistan.

Today, the Agricultural Development Bank of Pakistan has 355 branches and 51 regional offices in Pakistan. About 1,400 Mobile Credit Officers are engaged in the field to provide credit and technological services to farmers.

The breakdown of shareholders and their respective parts (in Pak. rupees million) is as follows:

State Bank of Pakistan	3,204.323
Government of Punjab	2.771
Government of Sindh	1.190
Government of N.W.F.P.	0.680
Government of Balochistan	0.359
Government of Erstwhile East Pakistan	5.000
Total	3,214.323

Table 7. Breakdown of shareholders of
Agricultural Development Bank of Pakistan

Chairman of the board of directors is Badruddin Zahidi.

There is no religious supervisory board, i.e. no shariah supervisory council.

(b) Objectives of the institution and services offered by the institution

One of Agricultural Development Bank of Pakistan's general objectives is to offer contemporary Islamic financial services. The bank provides credit to individual as well as corporate bodies engaged in agriculture and allied disciplines. It advances production and development loans and is playing a dominant role in the development of agriculture.

Agricultural Development Bank of Pakistan provides current and saving accounts as well as deposit accounts.

(c) Specifically religious business attitudes

Daily prayer times are practised. The period of fasting is kept. The client base is mixed; there are Muslims as well as non-Muslims.

(d) Future Outlook

Priorities in the future are the disbursement for agri-loans and the recoveries of the bank's dues.

(3) Industrial Development Bank of Pakistan

(a) General presentation of the institution

The Industrial Development Bank of Pakistan was established in Pakistan in August 1961.

There is an external supervisory body for Industrial Development Bank of Pakistan.

Today, the Industrial Development Bank of Pakistan has 19 offices in Pakistan.

The breakdown of shareholders and their respective parts is as follows: Federal Government and State Bank of Pakistan 92.9 % (56.59 % and 36.31 % respectively), others 7.1 %.

The bank was founded by the Federal Government.

Chairman and Managing Director is K M. Nagra. Executive Committee members are K M. Nagra, Javed Alam Khanzada and Capt. Farid-Un-Din Ahmed Zai.

There is no religious supervisory board, i.e. no shariah supervisory council.

(b) Objectives of the institution and services offered by the institution

Industrial Development Bank of Pakistan's general objectives are to offer contemporary Islamic financial services, to promote the Islamic economic and financial system and to fund development programs.

Industrial Development Bank of Pakistan provides current and saving accounts, deposit accounts, i.e. deposits of various maturities, letters of credit and guarantee and foreign ex-change services.

Since 1990-1991, Industrial Development Bank of Pakistan is also involved in leasing or *ijara*.

In its pursuit to introduce new instruments having Islamic financing features, a fully owned subsidiary of Industrial Development Bank of Pakistan was incorporated in January 1992 under the name Pakistan Industrial Financial Service (Pvt) Ltd, which is active in participation financing or *modaraba*

(c) Specifically religious business attitudes

Daily prayer times are practised. The period of fasting is kept.

The client base is almost 100 % Muslim.

(d) Future Outlook

There are new products being planned, which correspond to Islamic principles. Implementations in other locations and markets are also being planned. Priority is the collection of dues.

(4) Saudi-Pak Industrial & Agricultural Investment Company (PVT) Ltd

(a) General presentation of the institution

The Saudi-Pak Industrial & Agricultural Investment Company (PVT) Ltd was established in Pakistan in November 1981.

There is an external supervisory body for Saudi-Pak Industrial & Agricultural Investment Company (PVT) Ltd, namely 1. the State Bank of Pakistan, and 2. the Saudi Monetary Agency.

Today, the Saudi-Pak Industrial & Agricultural Investment Company (PVT) Ltd has one office in Pakistan.

The breakdown of shareholders and their respective parts is as follows: The governments of the Islamic Republic of Pakistan and of the Kingdom of Saudi Arabia each hold 50 % of the shares.

Founder members are the government of the Kingdom of Saudi Arabia and the government of the Islamic Republic of Pakistan.

Chairman of the board of directors is Dr. Saleh H. Humaidan, deputy chairman is Mohammad Javed Masud.

Management includes Muhammad Rashid Zahir (General Manager and Chief Executive) and Zaigham M. Rizvi (Senior Executive Vice President).

There is no religious supervisory board, i.e. no shariah supervisory council.

(b) Objectives of the institution and services offered by the institution

Saudi-Pak Industrial & Agricultural Investment Company (PVT) Ltd's general objective according to the mission statement is the strengthening of the economic co-operation between the people of Saudi Arabia and Pakistan by making investments in industrial including agro-based projects, and participating in investment related business in Pakistan. It aims at offering contemporary Islamic financial services, doing its business in compliance with the rules of Shariah, promoting the Islamic economic and financial system and funding development programs.

Saudi-Pak Industrial & Agricultural Investment Company (PVT) Ltd is active in commercial loans and letters of credit and guarantee.

The company is also involved in leasing or *ijara* and in sale and resale financing or *morabaha*.

Saudi-Pak Industrial & Agricultural Investment Company (PVT) Ltd is active in participation financing or *modaraba*, as well as in mutual participation financing or *musharaka*.

(c) Specifically religious business attitudes

Daily prayer times are practised. The period of fasting is kept.

The client base is mixed; there are Muslims as well as non-Muslims.

(d) Future Outlook

There are new products being planned. Priorities are to establish the company in Investment Banking and to raise foreign currency deposits from abroad in order to use currencies equivalents in long term and short term industrial projects.

(5) First Women Bank Limited

(a) General presentation of the institution

The First Women Bank Limited was established in Pakistan in December 1989.

There is an external supervisory body for First Women Bank Limited, namely the State Bank of Pakistan and the Government of Pakistan.

Today, the First Women Bank Limited has 36 branches, four general manager offices and the central office in a total of 21 towns in Pakistan.

The breakdown of shareholders and their respective parts is as follows: there is a consortium of five leading banks of the country. The government also has contributed to its equity:

Habib Bank Ltd.	31.65 %
Muslim Commercial Bank Ltd.	31.65 %
National Bank of Pakistan	10.55 %
United Bank Ltd.	10.55 %
Allied Bank of Pakistan	10.60 %
Ministry of Women Development	5.00 %
Total	100.00 %

Table 8. Breakdown of shareholders of
First Women Bank Limited

The Board of Directors consists of the presidents or directors of the shareholding parties.

There is no religious supervisory board, i.e. no shariah supervisory council.

(b) Objectives of the institution and services offered by the institution

First Women Bank Limited's general objectives according to the mission statement are to offer contemporary Islamic financial services, to promote the Islamic economic and financial system and to fund development programs. It aims at contributing for enhancing socio-economic status of women in Pakistan by activating them in economic process through special credit schemes and related facilities.

First Women Bank Limited provides current and saving accounts, deposit accounts, commercial loans, letters of credit and guarantee and foreign exchange services.

First Women Bank Limited is also involved in advance payment sale or *salam* and sale and resale financing or *morabaha*.

First Women Bank Limited considers that investment in conventional national and international equities is permitted, but so far the bank has not participated in such programmes.

(c) Specifically religious business attitudes

Daily prayer times are practised. The period of fasting is kept. Since its a Muslim women bank care is taken that dresses worn by staff should be according to Islamic principles.

The client base is Muslim and consists of about 7,000 women.

(d) Future Outlook

For 1997, there are plans to finance at least 70 projects on a *musharaka* basis. The priority is to finance at least 16 new businesses of women including funds not exceeding two million Pak. rupees on a mark up basis. But gradually, in 1997 some of the projects would be financed on a profit and loss sharing or *musharaka* basis as an experiment.

D. Co-operative banking

The banks included in this section will be presented in two groups: the first group represents Co-operative banking in Europe, the second one gives on indication of Co-operative banking in the Muslim World.

Co-operative banks in Europe will be presented in three sub-groups:

1. Banks which were founded by people of ethical motivation based on the religion of their environment will be presented in the group *banks of ethical origin*.

   This group includes DG Bank, Berliner Volksbank eG, Frankfurter Volksbank eG, Südwestbank AG and Deutsche Apotheker- u. Ärztebank eG.[85]

2. Banks which were not only founded by people of ethical motivation based on the religion of their environment, but they still support the work of the church today will be presented in the group *religion guided banks*.

   In this group, the Bank für Kirche und Diakonie eG and the Evangelische Darlehns-genossenschaft eG are analysed.

3. Banks which do not refer to religion *directly* are referred to as *non-religious ethical banks*.

   Here, Crédit Coopératif, The Co-operative Bank and the National Federation of Credit Unions are presented.

---

[85] *DG Bank* or Deutsche Genossenschaftsbank stands for "German co-operative bank", *Volksbank* in German means "popular bank", *Apotheker- u. Ärztebank* means "bank of pharmacists and doctors".

1. Co-operative banking in Europe

a) Banks of ethical origin

(1) DG Bank

(a) General presentation of the institution

The DG Bank was established in Germany in 1895.

The initial ideas came from Friedrich Wilhelm Raiffeisen and Hermann Schulze from Delitzsch who noticed the negative effects of the industrial revolution in Germany.

Today, the DG Bank has one head office and 22 branch offices in Germany.

It is part of the German co-operative banking structure with the following components:

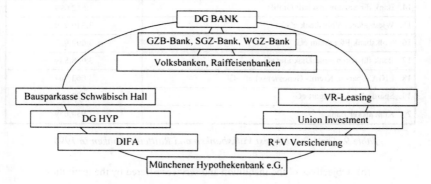

Illustration 12. DG Bank as head of the
German co-operative banking structure

In 1995, the Handelsblatt worked on a ranking of the 1,000 biggest Volksbanken and Raiffeisenbanken, with the following result:[86]

---

[86] Source: Handelsblatt 1995.

	Name of the bank	Balance 1994 in DM 000
1.	Deutsche Apotheker- u. Ärztebank eG	20,556,898
2.	Berliner Volksbank eG	15,301,410
3.	Badische Beamtenbank eG	7,709,428
4.	Grundkredit-Bank eG	6,403,723
5.	Evangelische Darlehnsgenossenschaft eG	5,333,026
6.	Stuttgarter Bank	4,978,220
7.	Südwestbank AG	4,972,423
8.	Frankfurter Volksbank eG	4,711,054
9.	Evangelische Kreditgenossenschaft eG	4,387,611
10.	Sparda-Bank Mainz eG	3,930,637
11.	Mainzer Volksbank eG	3,752,628
12.	Ulmer Volksbank eG	3,645,906
13.	Volksbank Baden-Baden * Rastatt eG	3,635,366
14.	Bank für Sozialwirtschaft GmbH	3,552,699
15.	Wiesbadener Volksbank eG	3,349,920
16.	Volksbank Pforzheim eG	3,092,927
17.	Bank für Kirche und Diakonie eG	3,068,839
18.	LIGA, Spar- u. Kredit- Genossenschaft eG	3,063,904
19.	Sparda-Bank Stuttgart eG	3,023,313
20.	Köpenicker Bank	2,934,059

Table 9. The 1,000 biggest Volksbanken and Raiffeisenbanken in 1995

(b) Objectives of the institution and services offered by the institution

DG Bank's general objectives are to offer contemporary financial services, especially to the German small and medium-sized companies, and to promote the co-operative economic and financial system.

DG Bank is active in commercial loans, letters of credit and guarantee and foreign exchange services.

DG Bank is also involved in leasing and offers investment funds.

(c) Specifically religious business attitudes

There are no specifically religious business attitudes.

(d) Future Outlook

There are new products being planned, i. e. electronic banking, credit cards and consultancy services. There are new implementations in other locations planned. Internationalisation is focused by the opening of representative offices in Shanghai and Bombay in 1995.

(2) Berliner Volksbank eG

(a) General presentation of the institution

Predecessors banks of the Berliner Volksbank eG were established in Germany in 1858, the bank itself in 1946.

It followed the ups and downs of German post-war history: In 1948, the bank was split in two de facto due to the separation of the economy; a formal decision followed in 1951. Ten years later, due to the construction of the Berlin wall, all organisational and personal links had to be given up. The eastern part became a socialist co-operative. After the fall of the wall, the two parts became reintegrated.

There is an external supervisory body for Berliner Volksbank eG, namely the Bundesanstalt für das Kreditwesen.

Today, the Berliner Volksbank eG has 79 offices in Berlin and the surrounding region.

There are more than 90,000 shareholders.

Management and board members are Ulrich Misgeld, Rudolf Prast and Jörn-Michael Gauss.

(b) Objectives of the institution and services offered by the institution

Berliner Volksbank eG's general objectives are to offer contemporary financial services and to promote the co-operative economic and financial system.

Berliner Volksbank eG is active in private banking, provides current and saving accounts, different types of deposit accounts, commercial loans and foreign exchange services.

(c) Specifically religious business attitudes

There were no such attitudes reported.

(d) Future Outlook

There are new products being planned, i. e. according to customer requests. There are no plans for the implementation in other locations or markets.

(3) Frankfurter Volksbank eG

(a) General presentation of the institution

The Frankfurter Volksbank eG has 65 offices in mostly in Frankfurt and the surrounding region.

The breakdown of shareholders and their respective parts is as follows: 61,210 members hold 741,687 parts of 100 DM each.

Management and board members are Albert Wehler, Walter Bühl, Heinz Sohn and Hans-Joachim Tonnellier.

(b) Objectives of the institution and services offered by the institution

Frankfurter Volksbank eG's general objectives are to offer contemporary financial services and to promote the co-operative economic and financial system.

Frankfurter Volksbank eG is active in private banking and provides current, saving and deposit accounts.

(c) Specifically religious business attitudes

There were no such attitudes reported.

(d) Future Outlook

There are new products being planned, i. e. new distribution channels, higher quality of advice, telephone and computer banking.

(4) Südwestbank AG

(a) General presentation of the institution

The Südwestbank AG was established in Germany in 1922.

Today, the Südwestbank AG has one head office and 51 branch offices in Stuttgart and the surrounding region.

The breakdown of shareholders and their respective parts is as follows: GZB-Bank owns 25 % of the shares, the rest is distributed to a larger public.

Management and board members are Dr. Peter Baumeister, Waldemar Fellmeth, Hans Bernd Röttgermann and Günter Sing.

(b) Objectives of the institution and services offered by the institution

Südwestbank AG's general objectives are to offer contemporary financial services. The initial objective was to give Raiffaisen banks access to business which was not allowed to them. After the merger of Volksbanken and Raiffaisen banks, this is not necessary any more.

Today, the bank wants to be a 'normal, regional bank'. It is in a somewhat ambiguous situation: On the one hand, the bank is still part of the German co-operative system - even one of the biggest elements as the table on page 102 shows. On the other hand, its organisation is as close to a conventional bank as possible.

The bank is active in private banking, provides current and saving accounts, deposit accounts, commercial loans and foreign exchange services.

Südwestbank AG is also involved in leasing and offers investment funds.

(c) Specifically religious business attitudes

There is no influence of religion on today's business of the bank. However it is recognised by the bank that Raiffaisen promoted the idea of co-operative banking with a Christian motivation.

(d) Future Outlook

There are new products being planned. Priority is given to the development towards a standard conventional bank.

(5) Deutsche Apotheker- u. Ärztebank eG

(a) General presentation of the institution

The Deutsche Apotheker- u. Ärztebank eG was established in Germany in 1902.

The bank was founded by 18 pharmacists in Danzig. Two years later, the first subsidiary was opened in Berlin. In 1907, the co-operative had 1,000 members already. After World War I, the headoffice was moved to Berlin. During the Nazi regime, the bank had to merger with the second pharmacist's bank, the "Spar- und Kreditverein Deutscher Apotheker m.b.H.". At the end of the war, the bank had to stop its activities due to allied law.

It was in 1948, that the newly formed "Westdeutsche Apotherkerbank e.G.m.b.H." could start its operations. In 1955, the dormant bank founded in 1902 was taken over, and finally in 1957, the new name "Deutsche Apotheker- u. Ärztebank eG " was approved. Since that time, there was a continuous financial growths. In 1990, 10 subsidiaries in East-Germany were opened.

Today, the Deutsche Apotheker- u. Ärztebank eG has one head office and 55 branch offices in all over Germany.

The breakdown of shareholders is as follows: there are 82,400 shareholders.

Management and board members are Richard Deutsch, Jürgen Helf, Bruno Nösser, Günter Preuß, Rudolf Reil and Werner Wimmer.

(b) Objectives of the institution and services offered by the institution

Deutsche Apotheker- u. Ärztebank eG's general objectives are to offer contemporary financial services to a specific customer group, i.e. pharmacists, doctors and dentists.

Deutsche Apotheker- u. Ärztebank eG is active in private banking, provides current and saving accounts, deposit accounts, commercial loans, letters of credit and guarantee and foreign exchange services.

Deutsche Apotheker- u. Ärztebank eG is also involved in leasing and offers investment funds. The institution also provides management consultancy for pharmacists.

(c) Specifically religious business attitudes

There were no such attitudes reported. As the client base consists of pharmacists and doctors only one could argue that the bank's clients have high professional ethics; however, this was not confirmed by the bank.

(d) Future Outlook

There are new products being planned. Special emphasis is given to home banking and consulting services.

b) Religion guided banks

(1) Bank für Kirche und Diakonie eG

(a) General presentation of the institution

The Bank für Kirche und Diakonie eG was established in Germany in 1953.

In 1991, the bank merged with the Bank für Kirche und Diakonie eG Berlin, which had been an independent successor of a credit co-operative formed in 1927.

Today, the Bank für Kirche und Diakonie eG has three offices in Berlin, Magdeburg and Duisburg.

The breakdown of shareholders is as follows: the bank is owned by 2,517 legal entities of church and social welfare work.

Director of the executive board is Dr. Nikolaus Becker.

Directors of the supervisory board is Heinz Pohlmann.

(b) Objectives of the institution and services offered by the institution

The Bank für Kirche und Diakonie eG's general objectives are to offer contemporary financial services to the church and its institutions, and to promote the co-operative economic and financial system.

The bank is active in private banking, provides current and saving accounts, deposit accounts, letters of credit and guarantee and foreign exchange services.

The Bank für Kirche und Diakonie eG also provides a *Diakoniesparbrief*. It is a fund for which no interest is paid to the customer but to maintain the capital value. Funds are used for social welfare work of the church or one of its institutions.

(c) Specifically religious business attitudes

There are business attitudes related to religion in that the annual report provides not only financial information but also information about the activities of the church. The bank is also reflecting on the role of money for the church and thus on its own role:

It recognises the tension between Jesus call to do missionary work and today's situation in which money is necessary to do this work, because the church owns church buildings that have to be maintained and employs priests that have to be paid. The bank apologises in saying that Jesus has paid the temple's tax himself and refers to those parts of the bible in which payment of interest is justified.

The institution concludes in saying that

- the church is doing its work in this world and therefore participates in social and economic life while accepting a special responsibility,

- financial activities of the church have to be measured against the bible and not only against economic pressures, which implies that the church will become guilty in economic life and therefore has to give special attention to social activities, and that

- the church has to focus its activities on the support of the poor and not on itself and the life of the institution.

It should be noticed that in addition to the arguments mentioned by the church, the institution also achieves a certain position of power by means of its business activities.

The client base is made up of about 2500 legal entities of the Christian church and social welfare work.

(d) Future Outlook

There are new products being planned. Implementations in other locations and markets is restricted by statutes.

(2) Evangelische Darlehnsgenossenschaft eG

(a) General presentation of the institution

The Evangelische Darlehnsgenossenschaft eG was established in Germany in 1968.

There is an external supervisory body for Evangelische Darlehnsgenossenschaft eG, namely the Norddeutscher Genossenschaftsverband.

Today, the Evangelische Darlehnsgenossenschaft eG has two offices, one in Kiel and one in Berlin.

The breakdown of shareholders is as follows: There are 1,972 members holding 166,542 shares totalling 49,962,600 DM.

The bank was founded by the Schleswig-Holsteinische Landeskirche. Chairman and managing director for the first 28 years was Erwin Köpke; he is succeeded by Karl-Heinz Holst. Other members of the executive board include Dr. Dieter Radtke and Joachim Philippi. Chairman of the supervisory board is Dr. Klaus Blaschke.

(b) Objectives of the institution and services offered by the institution

Evangelische Darlehnsgenossenschaft eG's general objectives are to offer banking services to the church and its institutions and to promote the co-operative economic and financial system.

Evangelische Darlehnsgenossenschaft eG is active in private banking, provides current and saving accounts, several types of deposit accounts and letters of credit and guarantee.

Evangelische Darlehnsgenossenschaft eG is also involved in leasing.

(c) Specifically religious business attitudes

The bank is doing business for the welfare institutions of the church. Its objective is to do business in favour of these organisations.

The client base is total Christian.

(d) Future Outlook

There are new products being planned. Implementations in other locations and markets are not planned. The priority is to do banking operations in favour of the institutions of the church.

c) Non-religious ethical banks

(1) Crédit Coopératif

(a) General presentation of the institution

Crédit Coopératif has one head office in region of Paris and 46 subsidiaries.

Directors include Jean Frebourg, who is director of development.

(b) Objectives of the institution and services offered by the institution

Crédit Coopératif's general objectives are to offer contemporary financial services, to promote the co-operative economic and financial system and to fund development programs.

Crédit Coopératif is active in financing projects for the benefit of the underprivileged in France. The bank has also launched funds for humanitarian projects, namely "Faim et développement" in 1983 and "Epargne solidaire".

(c) Specifically religious business attitudes

The bank works closely together with the catholic church in numerous projects of solidarity.

The client base is catholic to a large extend, but no precise record is kept of religious affiliations.

(d) Future Outlook

There are new products being planned, i. e. products helping the poor and the underprivileged.

110

(2) The Co-operative Bank

(a) General presentation of the institution

The Co-operative Bank was established in UK in 1872. The initial ideas came from Robert Owen, an industrialist and social reformer. The bank traces its origins back to the formation of the Loan and Deposit Department of the Co-operative Wholesale Society CWS. Only short time after 1872, it opened branches in Newcastle, London and Glasgow. After World War I, outlets were installed in stores of the CWS.

In 1972, when the bank had 32 branches, it changed its name to The Co-operative Bank. Three years later, it was the first bank for over 40 years to become a member of the Committee of London Clearing Banks, which was the starting point for rapid growth.

Today, the Co-operative Bank has 130 branches and over 2,600 automatic banking facilities in United Kingdom.

It is part of the British co-operative infrastructure, which also includes the "National Federation of Credit Unions", "CDS Co-operative Housing" and "Industrial Common Ownership Finance".

Managing director is Tom Agar.

(b) Objectives of the institution and services offered by the institution

The Co-operative Bank's general objectives are to offer contemporary financial services and to promote the co-operative economic and financial system. It wants to offer services to individual customers as well as to local authorities, businesses and the retail co-operative movement.

The Co-operative Bank is active in private banking, provides current and saving accounts, deposit accounts and foreign exchange services.

The bank also offers investment funds.

(c) Specifically religious business attitudes

According to the mission statement, the bank is non-partisan in all religious matters. However, it supports charity funds and gives support to the Christian aid weeks.

No record is kept of the religious affiliation of customers.

(d) Future Outlook

There are new products being planned, i. e. products corresponding to ethical criteria. Priority is given to the implementation of the ethical stance launched in 1992.

(3) National Federation of Credit Unions

(a) General presentation of the institution

The National Federation of Credit Unions was established in UK in 1964.

Today, the National Federation of Credit Unions has one office in Tyne & Wear, United Kingdom.

The shares of the institution belong to 120 regional credit unions.

The board of directors has 16 members.

(b) Objectives of the institution and services offered by the institution

National Federation of Credit Union's general objectives are to promote the co-operative economic and financial system and to fund development programs.

The federation is an advisory only. It is not a bank, and is forbidden to undertake banking services.

(c) Specifically religious business attitudes

There are no specifically religious business attitudes.

The client base is made of 35,000 members of its 120 credit unions. No distinction is made on the basis of religion and no record is kept of religious affiliations..

(d) Future Outlook

In the years to come, an image update is planned. Priorities is given to training.

2. Co-operative banking in the Muslim World

Grameen Bank

(a) General presentation of the institution

The Grameen Bank was established in Bangladesh in 1983 by Professor Muhammad Yunus, who wanted to overcome poverty with the help of the pooor.

Today, the Grameen Bank has one head office, 11 zonal offices, 100 area offices, 1,055 branches and 61,099 centres consisting of six groups in each centre with five members in each group in Bangladesh. It has become an internationally recognised successful development project.

The breakdown of shareholders and their respective parts is as follows: the borrowers, i.e. the poor people of Bangladesh, own 90 % of the shares, while the government owns 10 %.

Managing director is the founder Professor Muhammad Yunus.

(b) Objectives of the institution and services offered by the institution

Grameen Bank's general objective is to overcome poverty with the help of the poor people. The bank wants to establish credit as a human right.

Grameen Bank has established a way to do the business which differentiates it from conventional banks, but also from development organisations. Its key features are:

- the institutions provides credit - no charity, exclusively for the poor (women) in order to generate income, delivering its service at the doorstep.

- Procedures are simple, repayments are small.

- The business is done in small self-selected centres based in the villages and accompanied by a borrower-initiated social development programme.

- Saving is a priority. Members are obliged to weekly personal savings. There is also a group tax of 5 % of the loan amount collected for the group fund. In addition, an emergency fund is filled by contributions of 25 % of the interest payment from individual borrowers. It belongs to centres and can be taped in cases of emergency

113

like flood, fire or disease. All five group members must deposit savings before the first two applicants obtain loans.

(c) Specifically religious business attitudes

The concentration on the women population is linked to the fact that women are largely excluded from business due to the interpretation of Islamic law. Professor Yunus applied the co-operative approach to fight against poverty with his conviction that women are more long-term oriented than men and therefore have a preference for investment rather than consumption. This made them most promising partners in his work. In order to insert women in business in an Islamic environment, credit is delivered at the doorstep. More than 90 % of the bank's clients are female.

Credits have to be paid back with interest that is in accordance to local attitudes. The interdiction of *riba* is understood as an interdiction of excessive interest while a "normal" interest is considered to be allowed.

The client base is mostly Muslim.

(d) Future Outlook

There are new products being planned. Most important in the future is the implementation in other countries. Replicating the enormous success of Grameen Bank in other countries is a priority to the bank and has supporters as different as the German federal government and the Islamic Economic Development Foundation.

E. Synthesis and results

There is an influence of religion, i.e. of Christian Faith and Islam, on business ethics, i. e. in different modes of operation in the banking sector. This influence is varying.

1. Europe: Co-operative banking versus Islamic banking

In Europe, *Co-operative banking* exists for more than 100 years. Today, a differentiation can be observed: Some banks try to become as similar to conventional banks as possible, others stay with their Christian roots, yet others try to become non-religious ethical banks. The fact that the initial objective, overcoming poverty, has largely been achieved in Europe, may have contributed to this development.

Islamic banking is always only one part of the financial industry. Interestingly, there are Arab banks with subsidiaries in Europe providing Islamic banking services in specialist interest-free departments.

2. Muslim World: Co-operative banking versus Islamic banking

In the Muslim World, *Co-operative banking* is still relatively new and not to far away from its initial goal to overcome poverty.

Islamic banking exists beside co-operative and conventional banking, but there are also *totally* Islamic banking industries, e. g. in Pakistan. The Islamisation is as good an example for the *political support* of Islamic concepts which is also manifested in supra-national government banks.

3. Islamic banking: Europe versus the Muslim World

In terms of **geographical area of activity**, the Dar Al-Maal Al-Islami (DMI) Trust was chosen as an example for Islamic banking in **Europe** because of its administrative head office being in Switzerland, even though it also has numerous activities in the Muslim World. DMI defines itself as a "bridge" between Europe and the Muslim World. In terms of its business operations, no significant differences towards other Islamic banks could be observed. It seems reasonable to argue that the concept of Islamic banking has more influence on this bank than the environmental culture.

With regards to Islamic Banking in the **Muslim World**, a number of sub-groups of organisations were formed.

- The first group is made of *supra-national government banks*. This group illustrates political attempts to increase the influence of Islam on business practice by the Islamic Development Bank.

- The following two groups include *trusts involved in Islamic Banking*. Examples of concentration of power focusing on Islamic thought can be found here.

- In a third group, *local Islamic banks* are summarised. This shows how religion influences ways of conducting businesses that can neither recur on political nor on economic strength in the way the other banks can.

- A fourth group was formed by *the case of Pakistan*. This country provides an excellent case study for the influence of religion on business ethics on a national level.

Throughout all examples of Islamic Banking it was found out that Islamic banks offer conventional banking products as well as specifically Islamic ones.

Funds-channelling products		Gathering of funds	
Ijara-Wa-Iktina	Lease purchase	Non-marketable modaraba	Certificates of deposits
Ijara	Leasing		
Istisna	Manufacturing	Takafol deposits	
Salam	Advance payment sale		
Morabaha	Sale & Resale, alternative to conventional riba-based loan	General investment / Deposit accounts	
Qard Hassan	Interest-free loan, emergency fund	Savings accounts	
Traditional equities			
Asset-based modaraba • restricted • unrestricted • Musharaka	• Participation financing • Mutual participation financing	Current accounts	

Table 10. Banking products provided by Islamic financial institutions

Other services include letters of credit (wakalah), provision of guarantees (kafalah), foreign exchange (sarf) and transfers.

Based on these findings, Islamic banks could be described as **conventional banks with some modifications** in the product range according to religious interdictions. This means that Islamic Banking should not be seen as totally innovative but more as adaptation of conventional banking practices to Muslim ethics.

A **precision was necessary for the term "Islamic banking"** in that it should only be used for banking following *Shariah* principles and not for Arab banks such as the Arab Banking Corporation, which are run by Muslims and originate from Islamic countries, but nevertheless operate as conventional banks. They are however important in that they administer important funds which belongs to Muslims who are potential customers of Islamic banks. They are also involved in Islamic banking through subsidiaries. It is interesting to note that they have gathered funds largely due to the export of petroleum.

The **export of petroleum** is not only a driving force behind the initial concentration of capital in the hands of Muslims. It is still today a major reason for financing potential of banks owned by Muslim and contributes predominantly to the funds used to promote Islamic banking. A good example is the Islamic Development Bank which is one of the largest OPEC aid institutions.

It is important to note that depending on whether a country is petroleum-exporting or not, there are very poor countries in the Muslim World which are therefore potential recipients of funds, while others are relatively wealthy.

In terms of **financial performance** it was found that Islamic banks are generally successful companies in terms of profit and growth. They have large funds under management. It is interesting to note that Islamic banks report much the same way conventional banks report on their operations. Proofs of Islamic accounting could not be found.

In terms of development of Islamic Banking, **several generations** of banks can be distinguished: the *Islamic Development Bank* corresponds to an early generation of banks. Only later, fundaments of *Islamic Banking trusts* were laid. Theses trust gave raise to numerous other banks in all parts of the Islamic World and also to incorporation of Islamic banks in Europe. There is even an example of a trust which is administered in Europe. The later has even more a linking function than the Islamic banks in Europe themselves. Islamic Banking trusts can be seen as think tanks providing consultancy services to the subsidiaries. Among *local Islamic banks*, there are two different generations to be distinguished, of which the second came into being by the support of the earlier generation of banks.

The *country study of Pakistan* suggests that **the importance of Islam in general and particularly in business is increasing**. The European perception that Islamisation is getting more aggressive would support this tendency, however, this should be balanced against the fact that Islamic Banking heavily relates to conventional banking which is far from Islamic fundamentalism.

In addition, it becomes clear that there is a link between an early decolonialisation and an early wish to establish banks corresponding to Islamic principles. In addition, in analysing the founding dates and the titles of banks in Pakistan, a certain order might come at sight which lets suppose that **the establishment of banks followed general political movements**:

The Muslim Commercial Bank was established in 1947, the Agricultural Development Bank of Pakistan and the Industrial Development Bank of Pakistan were established in 1961, the Saudi-Pak Industrial & Agricultural Investment Company (PVT) Ltd was established in 1981, and the First Women Bank Limited in 1989. This corresponds to more global events: turning away from Europe with its colonialist past and concentration on the Islamic identity in the late 1940ies and the 1950ies, emphasis on development policy in the 1960ies, the insight that this policy let into a dead end and another concentration on the own identity in the late 1970ies and early 1980ies, and finally the increasing importance of the women movement in the mid- to late 1980ies.

It came out that there are Islamic banks which are **actively in search of funds** which they want to use to fulfil the requests of their customers. This implies potential for co-operation between Islamic banks and not necessarily Islamic providers of capital.

In summary, Islamic banking exists in Europe and in parts of the Islamic World as partial phenomenon besides co-operative and conventional banks. Furthermore, it exists in parts of the Islamic World within a totally Islamic banking industry. Among Islamic banks, *supra-national government banks*, *trusts involved in Islamic Banking* and *local Islamic banks* can be differentiated.

The influence of Islam on this mode of operation is direct in that it tries to translate Islamic religious law directly into business reality. Islamic banking can therefore be described as rule-based. It uses innovative banking products, while processes are similar to conventional banking. It has to be distinguished from Arabic banking, which has its geographic origins in the Muslim World as well, but apart from this is conventional banking.

Islamic banking is an ethical system which can be shared fundamentally by Muslims only because it is built on Muslim faith (ad hypotheses 1 and 3).[87]

4. Co-operative banking: Europe versus the Muslim World

With regards to co-operative banking in **Europe**, three groups of organisations were formed according to their motivation:

1. The first consists of *banks of ethical origin*. These banks were founded by people of ethical motivation based on the religion of their environment. The objective is to overcome poverty and to develop more justice in business life. Today, these roots are less and less important and banks develop towards conventional banks.

2. The second group consists of *religion guided banks*. These banks were not only founded by people of ethical motivation based on the religion of their environment, but they still support the work of the church today.

3. Finally, there are *non-religious ethical banks*. This title only means that these banks do not refer to religion directly. They provide added value to their customers by adhering to some form of formulated ethical policy. This policy is often directly inspired by the religion of the environment of the bank.

The only example of Co-operative banking in the **Muslim World** included in this study is Grameen Bank, which is sufficient in that Grameen Bank has served as a model for numerous other Co-operative banks in that area.

There are numerous similarities between co-operative banking in the Muslim world today and the early days of co-operative banking in Europe: there is an individual that takes the initiative to fight against injustice and exploitation of a large group of underprivileged workers by a small group of rich traders. The problem in both cases was the lack of working capital. It was not the consequences which were addressed by donations, but the cause which was addressed by an alternative way of credit allocation.

---

[87] Cf. page 67.

In terms of **financial performance** it was found that co-operative banks are generally successful companies in terms of profit and growth.

Co-operative banks seem to go through a **life cycle** and can be classified according to their date of foundation:

1. At the *starting point*, they are founded by people of ethical motivation based on the religion of their environment. The objective is to overcome poverty and to develop more justice in business life.

2. At some *recessionary point*, these primary objectives are more or less fulfilled: The socio-economic situation of the people who have dealt with co-operative banks has improved so much that the question can be asked whether the institutions can still justify their existence. Some banks continue to work the way they worked before, while others try to get as close to conventional banks as possible.

3. Later, a *second youth* can begin in the life cycle: the bank concentrates on its core competence, which is ethical banking. It reaffirms its position as an institution providing added-value and adapts to the new, wealthy environment.

The classifications can be integrated as follows:

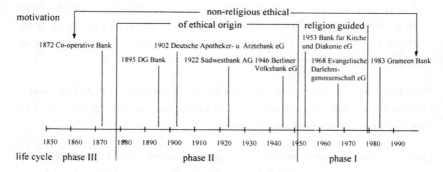

Illustration 13. Classification of co-operative banks

In summary, co-operative banking exists in Europe and the Muslim World as additions to conventional banks only. The influence of Christian Faith on this mode of operation in Europe and of Islam on this mode in the Muslim World is indirect, because it aims at the religious-determined objective to help the very poor. Co-operative banking can therefore described as outcome focused.

The influence of Christian Faith on co-operative banks in **Europe** is indirect, because Christian religion provides only the objective 'to help the poor', but not the way how to do this.

Similarly, the influence of Islam on co-operative banks in the **Muslim World** is indirect, because Muslim religion also provides only the objective 'to help the poor', but not the way how to do this.

Co-operative banking uses innovative business processes, while products are similar to conventional financial products.

It can therefore be described as a system in which Christians and Muslims share the same ethical principles in that they share the objective to care for their neighbour and to overcome poverty (ad hypotheses 2 and 3).[88]

F. Conclusions and further research

Conclusions

It was found that

- **Christian Faith** influences business ethics e.g. in the co-operative banking system, in which some banks are founded by Christians. Today, this influence is often merely a historic fact and only influences day-to-day business in some particular cases (ad hypothesis 2),

- **Islam** influences business ethics e.g. in the co-operative banking system, in which some banks are founded by Muslims, and in the Islamic banking system (ad hypotheses 1 and 2).

The potential strength of Islamic banks lays in the fact that they can serve a niche market in a very efficient way. With Islamic ethics as a basis they create value because they add meaning to the banking business: It is through them that the Coranic principles can be put into practice.

---

[88] Cf. page 67.

On the other hand, co-operative banks seem to have an answer to the fundamental problem of the majority of people in the majority of countries: They are able to provide working capital to people who do not possess anything or only a little more.

The potential strength of co-operative banks is also the implementation of meaning: Through them, global ethical standards can be put into practice. As they refer to fundamental rights of each human being, this concept is applicable on a global scale. Human rights can not be disqualified as a Western concept only, because an increasing number of Muslim theologians argues that human rights can be deducted from the Koran directly.

There are two possible fields of collaboration: In the co-operative banking sector, European banks could provide capital to its counterparts in the Muslim World in order to finance development programs. Islamic Banks in Europe could provide risk capital to small innovative companies that have enormous difficulties to obtain such capital from conventional banks (ad hypothesis 4).

The first co-operative bankers in the West were profoundly Christian people. Also, co-operative bankers of today wanting to enable people to sell their labour or production results at reasonable prices might just provide another way of understanding the Koran (2:275):

> "Those who devour usury will not stand except as stands one whom the evil one by his touch hath driven to madness. That is because they say: 'Trade is like usury', but ALLAH hath permitted trade and forbidden usury. ..."

Further research

A challenge for further research could be to test whether there are significant differences within Europe if special attention is given to Eastern Europe. Similarly, it should be found out whether there are significant differences within the different parts of the Muslim World such as the Near and Middle East as opposed to Southeast Asia.

Furthermore, it should be verified whether European research results are valid in countries of very similar tradition such as North America or Australia.

Another interesting direction could be to enlarge the number of religions involved. Special attention should be given to the Eastern religions in von Glasenapp's definition: is it easier for supporters of closely related religions to work together, or for those farer away?

Finally, other global business sectors that are active in both the Christian and the Muslim tradition could be included in further comparisons, such as the oil industry.

The following graphical illustration shows the three dimensions (x, y and z) of further research:

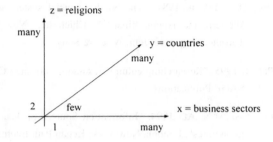

Illustration 14. Dimensions of further research

The oil industry might be a particularly interesting area of research, because it poses particular ethical problems, not only concerning the environment: there are sincere international disputes over pricing, and people go to war over oil. What makes the oil industry particularly interesting is the fact that today, most of the oil reserves are in Muslim countries, while consumption takes mainly place in the West. It would therefore be interesting to analyse the oil industry as place of encounter of religions. It could allow to introduce an ethical dimension in this industry.

Extending the research to Asian countries might be very valuable because this is an area in which Islam plays an important role. Other religions such as Shintoism or Buddhism are also based there. As economic growth in Asia is high at the moment, important investments are undertaken by countries of a Christian tradition.

LIST OF REFERENCES

ABDEEN, ADNAN / DALE SHOOK 1984: "The Saudi financial system in the context of Western and Islamic finance"; Chichester, New York, Brisbane, Toronto, Singapore: John Wiley & Sons.

ALASUUTARI, PERTTI 1995: "Researching culture"; London, Thousand Oaks, New Delhi: SAGE Publications.

ALI, S. NAZIM / NASSEEM N. ALI 1994: "Information Sources on Islamic Banking and Economics"; London, New York: Kegan Paul International.

BAHSI, KADRI A. 1990: "Struktur des Bankwesens in der Türkei"; Frankfurt am Main: Fritz Knapp Verlag.

BALKIR, CANAN / ALLAN M. WILLIAMS 1993: "Turkey and Europe"; London: Pinter Publishers.

VON BARATTA, DR. MARIO (ED.) 1995: "Der Fischer Weltalmanach 1996"; Frankfurt am Main: Fischer Taschenbuch Verlag.

BEAUGÉ, GILBERT 1990: "Les Capitaux de l'Islam"; Paris: Presses du CNRS.

BENMANSOUR, HACÈNE 1994a: "L'économie musulmane et la justice sociale"; Paris: Dialogues Editions.

BENMANSOUR, HACÈNE 1994b: "Politique économique en Islam"; Paris: Al Qalam Editions.

BENMANSOUR, HACÈNE 1995: "L'Islam et le riba"; Paris: Dialogues Editions.

BINSWANGER, H. C. / H. FRISCH / H. G. NUTZINGER 1988: "Arbeit ohne Umweltzerstörung"; Frankfurt am Main: Fischer Taschenbuch.

BORTZ, JÜRGEN 1988 (3rd edition): "Statistik für Sozialwissenschaftler"; Berlin, Heidelberg, New York, London, Paris, Tokyo: Springer-Verlag.

BRAKELMANN, GÜNTER 1988: "Zur Arbeit geboren?"; Bochum: SWI-Verlag.

BRAKELMANN, GÜNTER 1994: "Die protestantischen Wurzeln der Sozialen Marktwirtschaft"; Gütersloh: Gütersloher Verlagshaus Mohn.

BROWN, LESLEY (ED.) 1993: "The New Shorter Oxford English Dictionary"; Oxford: Clarendon Press.

LA BRUSLERIE, HUBERT ET AL. 1992: "Ethique, Déontologie et Gestion de l'Entreprise"; Paris: Ed. Economica.

BÜSCHER, MARTIN / MICHAEL VON HAUFF 1993: "Development Aid between Cultural Encounter and General Conditions of Economic Policy"; *Economics*; Tübingen, 57-80.

CORBIN, HENRY 1986: "Histoire de la philosophie islamique"; Paris: folio essais.

DONALDSON, THOMAS 1989: "The Ethics of International Business"; New York / Oxford: Oxford University Press.

DÜLFER, EBERHARD 1992: "Internationales Management"; München, Wien: R. Oldenbourg.

FEREIDOUNI, DR. HUSSAIN 1984: "Lessons in Islamic Ethics"; Teheran: Foreign Dep. of Bonyad Be'that.

FREEMAN, R. EDWARD 1991: "Business Ethics"; New York / Oxford: Oxford University Press.

GAMBLING, TREVOR / RIFAAT AHMED ABDEL KARIM 1991: "Business and Accounting Ethics in Islam"; London: Mansell Publishing.

LE GAI EATON, CHARLES 1994: "Der Islam und die Bestimmung des Menschen (Islam and the Destiny of Man)"; München: Wilhelm Heyne Verlag.

GANDZ, J. / N. HAYES 1988: "Teaching business ethics"; *JoBE, Journal of Business Ethics*. No. 9, 657-669.

EL-GAWHARY, KARIM 1994: "Islamische Banken in Ägypten. Soziale Verantwortung oder 'parasitäres' Gewinnstreben?"; Berlin: Verlag Das Arabische Buch.

AL GHAZALI, MOHAMMAD 1993: "L'éthique du Musulman"; Paris: Al Qalam Editions.

VON GLASENAPP, HELMUTH 1994 (4th edition, first published 1963): "Die fünf Welt-religionen"; München: Wilhelm Heyne Verlag.

DER GNADENREICHE KORAN 1960: "Übersetzung von Max Henning"; Stuttgart: Philipp Reclam.

HAARMANN, MARIA 1995: "Der Islam: Ein historisches Lesebuch"; München: C. H. Beck'sche Verlagsbuchhandlung.

HANDELSBLATT 1995: "Handelsblatt-Dokumentation 1995 - 1000 Volksbanken und Raiffeisenbanken"; Düsseldorf, Frankfurt: Verlagsgruppe Handels-blatt.

HERMEL, PHILIPPE 1993: "Management Européen et International"; Paris: Gestion Economica.

HOFSTEDE, GEERT 1993: "Interkulturelle Zusammenarbeit"; Wiesbaden: Gabler.

HOMANN, KARL / FRANZ BLOME-DREES 1992: "Wirtschafts- und Unternehmensethik"; Göttingen: Uni-Taschenbücher.

HONNETH, AXEL 1995 (3rd edition): "Kommunitarismus"; Frankfurt am Main, New York: Campus.

INSTITUTE OF ISLAMIC BANKING AND INSURANCE 1995: "Encyclopaedia of Islamic Banking and Insurance"; London: Institute of Islamic Banking and Insurance.

THE INTERLINEAR NIV HEBREW-ENGLISH OLD TESTAMENT 1987: "Translation by John R. Kohlenberger III"; Grand Rapids, Michigan: The Zondervan Corpo-ration.

VON KELLER, EUGEN 1982: "Management in fremden Kulturen"; Bern, Stuttgart: Haupt.

KANT, IMMANUEL 1968: "Grundlegung zur Metaphysik der Sitten"; Berlin: Akademie-Textausgabe.

KHAN, MUHAMMAD AKRAM (ED.) 1992: "Economic Teachings of Prophet Muhammad"; Delhi: Noor Publishing House.

KIRCHENAMT DER EVANGELISCHE KIRCHE IN DEUTSCHLAND 1991: "Gemeinwohl und Eigennutz - Wirtschaftliches Handeln in Verantwortung für die Zukunft"; Gütersloh: Gütersloher Verlagshaus Mohn.

KLÖCKER, MICHAEL / MONIKA TWORUSCHKA / UDO TWORUSCHKA 1995: "Wörterbuch Ethik der Weltreligionen"; Gütersloh: Gütersloher Verlagshaus Mohn.

VAN KOOLWIJK, JÜRGEN / MARIA WICKEN-MAYSER 1974: "Techniken der empirischen Sozialforschung"; München.

LEHRSTUHL FÜR ALLGEMEINE BETRIEBSWIRTSCHAFTSLEHRE UNIVERSITÄT ERLANGEN-NÜRNBERG 1994: "Unternehmensführung in Forschung und Lehre"; Nürnberg: Lehrstuhl für Allgemeine Betriebswirtschaftslehre Universität Erlangen-Nürnberg.

LÖHR, ALBERT / SUSANNE KILIAN 1993: "Die moralische Urteilskraft von Wirtschaftsstudenten"; Nürnberg: Lehrstuhl für Allgemeine Betriebswirtschaftslehre Universität Erlangen-Nürnberg.

LUDLOW, PETER ET AL. 1994: "Europe and the Mediterranean"; London: Brassey's.

MAXEINER, RUDOLF, DR. GUNTHER ASCHHOFF, DR. HERBERT WENDT 1988: "Raiffeisen - Der Mann, die Idee, das Werk"; Wiesbaden: Deutscher Genossenschafts-Verlag.

THE MEANING OF THE HOLY QUR'ÀN 1995: "Translation and commentary by Abdullah Yusuf Ali"; Beltsville: Amana Corporation.

MOHN, REINHARD 1995: "Erfolg durch Partnerschaft"; Berlin: Siedler Verlag.

MOUSSÉ, JEAN 1993: "Ethique et entreprises"; Paris: Librairie Vuibert.

AN-NA'HIM, ABDULLAHI ET AL. 1995: "Human Rights and Religious Values"; Amsterdam: Editions Rodopi.

NOMANI, FARHAD / ALI RAHNEMA 1994: "Islamic Economic Systems"; London, New Jersey: Zed Books.

NOOR-EBAD, HAMIDULLAH 1988: "Islamische Banken in Theorie und Praxis sowie ihre Auswirkungen auf die finanzielle Ressourcenallokation"; Köln: Unpublished dissertation.

OXFORD ANALYTICA 1986: "Islam in Perspective"; Oxford: Oxford Analytica Limited.

PACKARD, DAVID 1995: "The HP Way"; New York: Harper.

PERVEZ, IMTIAZ AHMAD 1995: "The Financial Instruments used by Islamic Banks"; *New Horizon*; London. No. 45, 3-5.

RAIFFEISEN, FRIEDRICH WILHELM 1866 (facsimile): "Die Dahrlehenskassen-Vereine als Mittel zur Abhilfe der Noth der ländlichen Bevölkerung sowie auch der städtischen Handwerker und Arbeiter"; Neuwied.

RAWLS, JOHN 1972: "A Theory of Justice"; New York / Oxford: Oxford University Press.

REICHSGESETZBLATT I 1889: "Gesetz betreffend die Erwerbs- und Wirtschaftsgenossen-schaften"; Berlin, 55.

RICH, ARTHUR 1984: "Wirtschaftsethik I"; Gütersloh: Gütersloher Verlagshaus Mohn.

RICH, ARTHUR 1990: "Wirtschaftsethik II"; Gütersloh: Gütersloher Verlagshaus Mohn.

RODINSON, MAXIM 1991 (2nd edition): "Die Faszination des Islam (La fascination de l'Islam)"; München: Beck'sche Reihe.

ROUX, JANINE 1981: "Guides des religions"; Paris: Editions du Dauphin.

SCHIMMEL, ANNEMARIE 1990: "Der Islam. Eine Einführung"; Stuttgart: Philipp Reclam.

SCHMIDT-BRABANT, MANFRED 1995: "Spirituell verstandenes Bankwesen"; Dornach: Verlag am Goetheanum.

SEIFERT, EBERHARD K. 1989: "Hauptlinien im gegenwärtigen wirtschaftsethischen Diskurs"; *Wirtschaftsethik und ökologische Wirtschaftsforschung*; Bern / Stuttgart, 21-37.

SEN, AMARTYA 1994 (reprint of 1987): "On Ethics and Economics"; New York / Oxford: Blackwell.

SIDDIQI, MUHAMMAD NEJATULLAH 1988: "Banking without interest"; London: The Islamic Foundation.

SMITH, ADAM 1981 (first published 1776): "An Inquiry into the Nature and Causes of the Wealth of Nations"; Oxford: Clarendon Press.

SPÖHRING, W. 1989: "Qualitative Sozialforschung"; Stuttgart.

STAFFELBACH, BRUNO 1994: "Management-Ethik"; Bern, Stuttgart, Wien: Haupt.

STEINMANN, HORST / ALBERT LÖHR 1991 (2nd edition): "Unternehmensethik als Ordnungselement in der Marktwirtschaft"; Stuttgart: Lehrstuhl für Allgemeine Betriebswirtschaftslehre Universität Erlangen-Nürnberg.

STEINMANN, HORST / ALBERT LÖHR 1993 (2nd edition): "Grundlagen der Unternehmensethik"; Stuttgart: Schäffer-Poeschel.

STEINMANN, HORST / ALBERT LÖHR 1994: "Unternehmensethik - ein republikanisches Programm in der Kritik"; *Markt und Moral*; Bern, Stuttgart, Wien, 145-180.

STEMBERGER, GÜNTER 1995: "Die Juden: Ein historisches Lesebuch"; München: C. H. Beck'sche Verlagsbuchhandlung.

STIVERS, ROBERT L. ET AL. 1994: "Christian Ethics"; New York: Orbis Books.

TERWEY, MICHAEL 1994: "Pluralismus des Glaubens in der Diskussion"; *ZA-Information 35*; Köln, 110-134.

TROMPENAARS, FONS 1994: "L'entreprise multiculturelle (Riding the waves of culture.)"; Paris: Maxima.

ULRICH, PETER 1990: "Wirtschaftsethik als Kritik der "reinen" ökonomischen Vernunft"; *Ökonomie und Ethik*; Freiburg i. Br., 111-138.

ULRICH, PETER 1993: "Wirtschaftsethik als Beitrag zur Bildung mündiger Wirtschaftsbürger"; *Ethica*; Innsbruck. 1/1993, 227-250.

ULRICH, PETER / EDGAR FLURI 1992 (6th edition): "Management - Eine konzentrierte Einführung"; Bern / Stuttgart: Uni-Taschenbücher.

USUNIER, JEAN-CLAUDE 1992a: "Commerces entre cultures, tome 1"; Paris: Presses Universitaires de France.

USUNIER, JEAN-CLAUDE 1992b: "Commerces entre cultures, tome 2"; Paris: Presses Universitaires de France.

WEBER, MAX 1993 (first published 1904/05): "Die protestantische Ethik und der "Geist" des Kapitalismus"; Bodenheim: Athenäum Hain Hanstein.

WEILER, RUDOLF 1991: "Einführung in die katholische Soziallehre"; Graz, Wien, Köln: Styria.

WILSON, RODNEY 1993: "Equity finance of economic development"; *MFI, Managerial Finance*, 70-81.

ZUBAIDA, SAMI 1993: "Islam - The People & The State"; London, New York: I. B. Tauris.

NN 1987: "Ethik als Herausforderung für die Theorie und Praxis des Managements"; *Die Unternehmung*. 6/1987.

NN 1995: "Où est la banque islamique?"; *New Horizon*; London. No. 44, 2.

APPENDICES

Appendix A. Overview of Arabic terms

hajj	pilgrimage
ihsan	good behaviour towards the neighbour
ijara	leasing
ijara-wa-iktina	lease purchase
ikhlas	sincerely worshipping God
imam	leader of Muslim community
istisna	finance of manufacturing
massaref	Islamic banks
morabaha	sale and resale, alternative to conventional interest-based loans
mujtahidun	Muslim theological interpreter of the law
musharaka	mutual participation financing, variation of morabaha in which case the bank invests own capital in addition to the customers' capital
qard hassan	interest-free loans
ramadan	month of fasting
riba	interest, usury
ribh	profit
sadaqa	donations to the poor
salam	advance payment sale
shahada	Muslim confession
shariah	Muslim religious law
slat	prayer
takafol	Islamic solidarity insurance
tawakkul	trust in God
zakat	alms tax

Appendix B. Numeric comparisons

World Religions

There are widely differing estimations about the numerical distribution of religions in mankind. The following provides a comparison between the two (in millions):[89]

		Von Glasenapp	Von Baratta
A. Religions of nature			
1.	Primitive	120	N/A
2.	Shintoist	50	3
B. Eastern religions			
1.	Hindu	390	754
2.	Sikhs	7	18.8
3.	Jainas	1.5	3.8
4.	Buddhist (without Chinese)	200	300
5.	Chinese Universalists and Buddhists	500	N/A
C. Western religions			
1.	Zoroastrians	0.15	0.12
2.	Jews	12	17.8
3.	Christians: Roman Catholic	538	1 042.5
	Christians: Protestant	215	375
	Christians: Orthodox	120	173.5
	Christians: other	17	278.7
	Christians: total	890	1 869.7
4.	Muslims	430	971.3

As far as the Muslims are concerned, Oxford Analytica (1986, 12) estimates a total of 700 million Muslims in the world, out of which 87 million would be Shi'is .

---

[89] Von Glasenapp (1994, 412) has based his figures on estimations of a world population of 3,000 million. Von Baratta (1995, 1135-1142) estimates a world population of 5,716 millions. Numbers for Asia are particularly unreliable because people are possibly counted several times due to double confessions.

Europe and the Muslim World

The total population of the countries belonging to the Muslim World is 885,386,000, whereas the total European population amounts to 660,000,000 if the Muslim countries in Europe, Albania and Azerbaijan, are counted as part of the Muslim World.

The population of countries belonging to the Muslim World in the Near and Middle East is 206,045,000, in Africa 201,539,000, on the Indian Subcontinent 260,548,000, in Southeast Asia 206,472,000 and in Muslim countries in Europe 10,782,000. In detail, the distribution of the Muslim population by area is as follows:[90]

Near and Middle East

Country	Inhabitants	Country	Inhabitants
1. Bahrain	533,000	9. Saudi Arabia	17,392,000
2. Iran	64,169,000	10. Syria	13,696,000
3. Iraq	19,465,000	11. Turkey	59,597,000
4. Jordan	4,102,000	12. Turkmenistan	3,921,000
5. Kuwait	1,800,000	13. United Arab Emirates	1,807,000
6. Lebanon	3,855,000		
7. Oman	1,988,000	14. Yemen	13,196,000
8. Qatar	524,000		

---

[90] Cf. von Baratta (1995).

Africa

Country	Inhabitants	Country	Inhabitants
15. Algeria	26,722,000	23. Mali	10,135,000
16. Chad	6,010,000	24. Mauritania	2,161,000
17. Comoros	471,000	25. Morocco	25,954,000
18. Djibouti	557,000	26. Niger	8,550,000
19. Egypt	56,434,000	27. Senegal	7,902,000
20. Gambia	1,042,000	28. Somalia	8,954,000
21. Guinea	6,306,000	29. Sudan	26,641,000
22. Libya	5,044,000	30. Tunisia	8,656,000

Indian Subcontinent, Afghanistan and Kyrghyzstan

Country	Inhabitants	Country	Inhabitants
31. Afghanistan	17,691,000	34. Maldives	238,000
32. Bangladesh	115,200,000	35. Pakistan	122,829,000
33. Kyrghyzstan	4,590,000		

Southeast Asia

Country	Inhabitants	Country	Inhabitants
36. Brunei	274,000	38. Malaysia	19,047,000
37. Indonesia	187,151,000		

Muslim countries in Europe

Country	Inhabitants	Country	Inhabitants
39. Albania	3,398,000	40. Azerbaijan	7,384,000

Appendix C. Questionnaires

On the following pages, the two questionnaires used for the survey are presented.

1. The first questionnaire was sent to Muslim financial institutions. There was only one version of the questionnaire, which was in English. In the list of institutions covered by this research in "Appendix D." this questionnaire is referred to as "Q 1".

2. The second questionnaire was sent to co-operative financial institutions. As some of the German co-operative banks were willing to participate in the survey only if there was a German edition of the questionnaire, there is a German version in addition to the English one. In the list of institutions covered by this research in "Appendix D." this questionnaire is referred to as "Q 2".

Questionnaire (Q 1)

To: Ingmar M. Wienen
Address: Reinhardtstr. 11, D-10117 Berlin, Germany
Phone & Fax: (+49 30) 281 78 27

From:
Address:
Phone:
Fax:

Date:

Please take a moment.

Thank you for helping me in my research. Please indicate the answers and check one box for the questions where appropriate. Do not hesitate to use additional paper if necessary. I will handle sensitive information with care.

Could you provide me with your three latest company reports? If you have any other documentation about your company or the products and services you offer, I would also be pleased to obtain a copy.

1. Branches
1.1. Number of offices: _____

1.2. Number of locations / countries: _____

1.3. Addresses: _____

2. Date of formation, background
2.1. When established? _____
2.2. Ownership: breakdown of shareholders and
their respective parts: _____
2.3. Which Islamic principles are incorporated in
the state's law? _____

3. Founder members, directors, management and board members
3.1. Who are the founder members,
directors, management and board members? _____
3.2. Is there a religious supervisory board / Shariah
supervisory council? _____
3.3. Are there other supervisory bodies
such as government? _____

4. Objectives, areas of operation, services offered

4.1. Which general objectives are pursued?
- Offer contemporary Islamic financial services   ☐   YES   ☐   NO
- Compliance with rules of Shariah   ☐   YES   ☐   NO
- Promotion of
  Islamic economic and financial system   ☐   YES   ☐   NO
- Development programs   ☐   YES   ☐   NO
- Other: _____

4.2. Which banking operations and which specifically Islamic ones are done?
- Private banking   ☐   YES   ☐   NO
- Current and saving accounts   ☐   YES   ☐   NO
- Deposit accounts   ☐   YES   ☐   NO
  Which types of deposit accounts? _____
- Commercial loans   ☐   YES   ☐   NO
- Letters of credit and guarantee   ☐   YES   ☐   NO
- Foreign exchange services   ☐   YES   ☐   NO

- Leasing (*ijara*)   ☐   YES   ☐   NO
- Investment funds (*modaraba*)   ☐   YES   ☐   NO
  Restricted/unrestricted? _____
  Investment in traditional national
  and international equities permitted? _____
  Mutual participation financing   ☐   YES   ☐   NO
- Claims on income streams
  resulting from commercial transactions   ☐   YES   ☐   NO
- Claims concerning
  debts payable at certain future dates   ☐   YES   ☐   NO
  Financing resale of goods   ☐   YES   ☐   NO
  advance payment (*salam*)   ☐   YES   ☐   NO
  istisna   ☐   YES   ☐   NO
  qard hassan   ☐   YES   ☐   NO
- Participation financing leading to acquisition   ☐   YES   ☐   NO
- Other: _____

4.3. Which other business attitudes are specifically Islamic ones?
- Practice of daily prayer times   •   YES   ☐   NO
- Particularities during the period of fasting   •   YES   ☐   NO
- Other: _____

5. Capital structure, economic performance

5.1. Authorised share capital: _____

5.2. How much of the capital is issued / paid? _____

5.3. Assets -
cash & liquid funds, investments, other: _____

5.4. Liabilities - deposits, bonds & loan capital,
reserves, bills payable, other liabilities, profit: _____

5.5. Client base - total / Muslim / non-Muslim: _____

6. Future Plans

6.1. Are there new products being planned? _____

6.2. Implementations in other locations / markets? _____

6.3. Which are the priorities? _____

Other Comments

_____

_____

_____

_____

_____

_____

_____

Questionnaire (Q 2)

To: Ingmar M. Wienen
Address: Reinhardtstr. 11, D-10117 Berlin, Germany
Phone & Fax: (+49 30) 281 78 27

From:
Address:
Phone:
Fax:

Date:

Please take a moment.

Thank you for helping me in my research. Please indicate the answers and check one box for the questions where appropriate. Do not hesitate to use additional paper if necessary. I will handle sensitive information with care.

Could you provide me with your three latest company reports? If you have any other documentation about your company or the products and services you offer, I would also be pleased to obtain a copy.

1. Branches
1.1. Number of offices: _____

1.2. Number of locations / countries: _____

1.3. Addresses: _____

2. Date of formation, background
2.1. When established?   _____
2.2. Ownership: breakdown of shareholders and
     their respective parts: _____

3. Founder members, directors, management and board members
3.1. Who are the founder members,
     directors, management and board members?   _____
3.2. Which supervisory bodies
     exist?   _____

4. Objectives, areas of operation, services offered

4.1. Which general objectives are pursued?
- Offer contemporary financial services   ☐ YES   ☐ NO
- Promotion of
  co-operative economic and financial system   ☐ YES   ☐ NO
- Development programs   ☐ YES   ☐ NO
- Other: _____

_____

4.2. Which banking operations and which specifically co-operative ones are done?
- Private banking   ☐ YES   ☐ NO
- Current and saving accounts   ☐ YES   ☐ NO
- Deposit accounts   ☐ YES   ☐ NO
  Which types of deposit accounts?
- Commercial loans   ☐ YES   ☐ NO
- Letters of credit and guarantee   ☐ YES   ☐ NO
- Foreign exchange services   ☐ YES   ☐ NO

- Leasing   ☐ YES   ☐ NO
- Investment funds   ☐ YES   ☐ NO
  Restricted/unrestricted? _____
  Investment in traditional national
  and international equities permitted?
  Mutual participation financing   ☐ YES   ☐ NO
- Claims on income streams
  resulting from commercial transactions   ☐ YES   ☐ NO
- Claims concerning
  debts payable at certain future dates   ☐ YES   ☐ NO
  advance payment   ☐ YES   ☐ NO
- Participation financing leading to acquisition   ☐ YES   ☐ NO
- Other: _____

4.3. Are there business attitudes which have a religious background?

_____

_____

_____

5. Capital structure, economic performance

5.1. Authorised share capital: _____

5.2. How much of the capital is issued / paid? _____

5.3. Assets -
cash & liquid funds, investments, other: _____

5.4. Liabilities - deposits, bonds & loan capital,
reserves, bills payable, other liabilities, profit: _____

5.5. Client base - total / Christian / Muslim / other: _____

6. Future Plans

6.1. Are there new products being planned? _____

6.2. Implementations in other locations / markets? _____

6.3. Which are the priorities? _____

Other Comments

_____

_____

_____

_____

_____

_____

Appendix D. Institutions covered by this research

The following provides an overview of the institutions covered by this research. Copies of the first of the two questionnaires, presented as "Questionnaire (Q 1)", were sent to companies marked "Q 1", whereas copies of the second, presented as "Questionnaire (Q 2)", were sent to the other companies.

Companies marked "OK" replied to the request for information. Companies marked "DMI" belong to the Dar Al-Maal Al-Islami (DMI) Trust.

Out of 119 banks, 34 replied.

Q	OK	DMI	COMPANY	COUNTRY
Q 1	OK	DMI	Islamic Takafol and Retakafol (Bahamas) Company Ltd, Massraf Faysal Al-Islami Ltd	Bahamas
Q 1			Al Amin Securities Company, Al Tawfeek Company for Investment Funds	Bahrain
Q 1	OK		Albaraka Islamic Investment Bank	Bahrain
Q 1	OK		Bahrain Islamic Bank	Bahrain
Q 1			Bahrain Islamic Insurance Company BSC	Bahrain
Q 1		DMI	Faysal Islamic Bank of Bahrain E.C.	Bahrain
Q 1	OK	DMI	Islamic Investment Company of the Gulf (Bahrain) E.C.	Bahrain
Q 1			Islamic Leasing Company	Bahrain
Q 1		DMI	Takafol Islamic Insurance Company, Bahrain E.C.	Bahrain
Q 2	OK		Grameen Bank	Bangladesh
Q 1			Albaraka Bangladesh Ltd	Bangladesh
Q 1			Islamic Bank of Brunei Berhad	Brunei
Q 1			Islamic Bank International of Denmark	Denmark
Q 1			Banque Albaraka Djibouti	Djibouti
Q 1			Dubai Islamic Bank	Dubai
Q 1	OK		Faisal Islamic Bank of Egypt S.A.	Egypt
Q 1		DMI	Islamic Investment and Development Company	Egypt
Q 1			Islamic International Bank for Investment and Development	Egypt
Q 2	OK		Crédit Coopératif	France
Q 2			Badische Beamtenbank eG	Germany

142

Q	OK	DMI	COMPANY	COUNTRY
Q 2	OK		Bank für Kirche und Diakonie eG	Germany
Q 2			Bank für Sozialwirtschaft GmbH	Germany
Q 2	OK		Berliner Volksbank eG	Germany
Q 2	OK		Deutsche Apotheker- u. Ärztebank eG	Germany
Q 2	OK		DG Bank	Germany
Q 2	OK		Evangelische Darlehnsgenossenschaft eG	Germany
Q 2			Evangelische Kreditgenossenschaft eG	Germany
Q 2	OK		Frankfurter Volksbank eG	Germany
Q 2			Grundkredit-Bank eG	Germany
Q 2			Köpenicker Bank	Germany
Q 2			LIGA, Spar- u. Kredit- Genossenschaft eG	Germany
Q 2			Mainzer Volksbank eG	Germany
Q 2			Sparda-Bank Mainz eG	Germany
Q 2			Sparda-Bank Stuttgart eG	Germany
Q 2			Stuttgarter Bank	Germany
Q 2	OK		Südwestbank AG	Germany
Q 2			Ulmer Volksbank eG	Germany
Q 2			Volksbank Baden-Baden * Rastatt eG	Germany
Q 2			Volksbank Pforzheim eG	Germany
Q 2			Wiesbadener Volksbank eG	Germany
Q 1			Misr Bank Europe GmbH	Germany
Q 1			Massraf Faysal Al-Islami de Guinée	Guinea
Q 1			Al-Ameen Islamic Financial & Investment Corporation India Ltd	India
Q 1	OK		Bank Muamalat	Indonesia
Q 1			Bank Keshavarzi	Iran
Q 1			Bank Markazi Jomhouri Islami	Iran
Q 1			Bank Maskan	Iran
Q 1			Bank Mellat	Iran
Q 1			Bank Melli	Iran
Q 1			Bank Saderat	Iran
Q 1			Bank Sanat Va Maadan	Iran
Q 1			Bank Sepah	Iran
Q 1			Bank Tejarat	Iran
Q 1			Iraqi Islamic Bank for Investment and Development	Iraq
Q 1			Kuwait Finance House KSC	Kuwait

Q	OK	DMI	COMPANY	COUNTRY
Q 1		DMI	Faisal Finance (Luxembourg) S.A.	Luxembourg
Q 1		DMI	Takafol S.A.	Luxembourg
Q 1			Syarikat Takaful Malaysia Senderian Berhad	Malaysia
Q 1			Bank Bumiputra Malaysia Berhad	Malaysia
Q 1	OK		Bank Islam Malaysia Berhad	Malaysia
Q 1			Lembaga Ususan Dan Tabung Haji	Malaysia
Q 1	OK		Malayan Banking Berhad	Malaysia
Q 1			United Malayan Banking Corporation Berhad	Malaysia
Q 1			Malaysian National Insurance	Malaysia
Q 1			Koparski Pegawai-Pegawai Melayu Malaysia Berhad (MOCCIS)	Malaysia
Q 1			Bank Albaraka Mauritanienne Islamique	Mauritania
Q 1		DMI	Al-Faysal Investment Bank Ltd	Pakistan
Q 1			Allied Bank of Pakistan Ltd	Pakistan
Q 1			Bankers Equity Ltd	Pakistan
Q 1	OK		First Women Bank Ltd	Pakistan
Q 1			Bank Al Habib Bank Ltd	Pakistan
Q 1			House Building Finance Corporation	Pakistan
Q 1	OK		Industrial Development Bank of Pakistan	Pakistan
Q 1			Investment Corporation of Pakistan	Pakistan
Q 1			Khadim Ali Shah Bukhari & Co. Ltd	Pakistan
Q 1	OK		Muslim Commercial Bank	Pakistan
Q 1	OK		State Bank of Pakistan	Pakistan
Q 1			National Investment Trust Ltd	Pakistan
Q 1			Pakistan Industrial Credit & Investment Corporation Ltd	Pakistan
Q 1	OK		Saudi-Pak Industrial & Agricultural Investment Company (PVT) Ltd, Small Business Finance Corp.	Pakistan
Q 1	OK		United Bank Ltd	Pakistan
Q 1	OK		Agricultural Development Bank of Pakistan	Pakistan
Q 1			Qatar Islamic Bank (S.A.Q.)	Qatar
Q 1			Albaraka Investment & Development Company	Saudi Arabia
Q 1			Al Rajhi Banking & Investment Corporation	Saudi Arabia
Q 1	OK		Islamic Development Bank	Saudi Arabia
Q 1		DMI	Banque Islamique du Sénégal	Senegal
Q 1			Tadamon Islamic Bank	Sudan
Q 1			Albaraka Bank	Sudan

Q	OK	DMI	COMPANY	COUNTRY
Q 1			Faisal Islamic Bank of Sudan S.A.	Sudan
Q 1			Islamic Bank of Western Sudan	Sudan
Q 1			Islamic Co-operative Development Bank	Sudan
Q 1	OK	DMI	Faisal Finance (Switzerland) S.A.	Switzerland
Q 1	OK	DMI	Dar Al-Maal Al-Islami (DMI) Trust	Switzerland
Q 1	OK	DMI	Pan Islamic Consultancy Services Istishara S.A.	Switzerland
Q 1			Beit El Tamwil Saudi Tounsi, B.E.S.T. Bank	Tunisia
Q 1	OK		Faisal Islamic Bank of Kibris Ltd	Turkey
Q 1			Albarka Turkish Finance House	Turkey
Q 1		DMI	Faisal Finance Institution Inc.	Turkey
Q 2			Association of British Credit Unions	UK
Q 2	OK		CDS Co-operative Housing	UK
Q 2			Co-operative Insurance Society	UK
Q 2	OK		Industrial Common Ownership Finance	UK
Q 2			Industrial Common Ownership Movement	UK
Q 2	OK		National Federation of Credit Unions	UK
Q 2	OK		The Co-operative Bank	UK
Q 1			Albaraka Investment Company, London	UK
Q 1		DMI	Massraf Faysal Al-Islami Ltd, Jersey	UK
Q 1			Kleinwort Benson Ltd., Mrs Stella Cox	UK
Q 1			Citibank International plc, Mr Atiq Ur Rehman	UK
Q 1			Arbuthnot Latham & Co., Dr. Mohammad Abdel Haq	UK
Q 1	OK		ANZ International Merchant Banking, Mr. Adil Ahmed	UK
Q 1			Gulf International Bank BSC, Mr. R. Chattaway	UK
Q 1	OK		ABC International Bank plc, T. Pooley	UK
Q 1			IBJ International / Industrial Bank of Japan, Mr. Saad Raja	UK
Q 1			J. Aron & Co. / Goldman Sachs International, Mr. Roy Salamol	UK
Q 1			United Bank of Kuwait plc, Mr. Duncan Smith	UK
Q 1			Arab Bank plc, Mr. Iyad Quttaineh	UK
Q 1			Bank Ryadh, Miss Najma Al-Tunisi	UK

Appendix E. Highlights of the financial performance

In this section, highlights of the financial performance of the institutions covered by this research are presented.

1. Islamic banking in Europe

Dar Al-Maal Al-Islami (DMI) Trust

1. DMI headquarters and administration

For 1995, the following consolidated balance sheet provides an overview of the financial situation of Dar Al-Maal Al-Islami (DMI) Trust:

Assets $ 000		Liabilities $ 000	
Cash & liquid funds	613,235	Issued & paid-up capital	225,923
Investments	262,085	Current liabilities	557,256
Loans		Long-term liabilities	6,874
		Other liabilities	85,267
Total assets	875,320	Total liabilities	875,320

Table 11. 1995 Balance sheet of
Dar Al-Maal Al-Islami (DMI) Trust

Key financial figures on income (in $ 000) include:

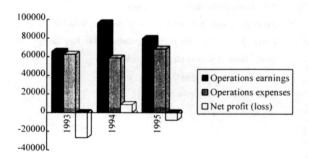

Illustration 15. 1993-1995 Income statements of Dar Al-Maal Al-Islami (DMI) Trust

2. Faisal Finance (Switzerland) S.A.

Authorised share capital is 20 million SFr, of which 100 % is issued. Equities total 32 million SFr, while funds under management are 730 million SFr.

3. Islamic Investment Company of the Gulf (Bahrain) E.C.

For 1995, the following consolidated balance sheet provides an overview of the financial situation of Islamic Investment Company of the Gulf (Bahrain) E.C.:

Assets $ 000		Liabilities $ 000	
Cash & liquid funds	10,487	Issued & paid-up capital	30,000
Due from related companies	2,986	Reserves	6,100
Investment in related comp.	2,258	Due to related companies	1,259
Islamic financing	4,500		
Short term investments	25,215	Other liabilities	11,473
Long term investments	15,750	Proposed dividend	10,000
Other	3,536	Profit / loss	5,900
Total assets	64,732	Total liabilities	64,732

Table 12. 1995 Balance sheet of
Islamic Investment Company of the Gulf (Bahrain) E.C.

Key financial figures on income include:

Illustration 16. 1992-1994 Income statements of
Islamic Investment Company of the Gulf (Bahrain) E.C.

147

4.   Islamic Takafol and Retakafol (Bahamas) Company Ltd

For 1994, the following consolidated balance sheet provides an overview of the financial situation of Islamic Takafol and Retakafol (Bahamas) Company Ltd:

Assets $		Liabilities $	
Cash & liquid funds	529,686	Authorised capital	25,000,000
Investments	11,325,500	Issued & paid-up capital	10,000,000
Receivable from *retakafol*	991,290	Accounts payable	33,459
Accrued income	150,509	Due to group companies	4,127
		Provisions	38,467
Other	26,838	Profit / loss	2,947,770
Total assets	13,023,823	Total liabilities	13,023,823

Table 13. 1994 Balance sheet of
Islamic Takafol and Retakafol (Bahamas) Company

Key financial figures on income include:

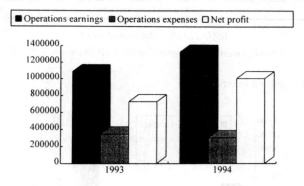

Illustration 17. 1993-1994 Income statements of the
Islamic Takafol and Retakafol (Bahamas) Company Ltd

2. Islamic banking in the Muslim World

a) Supra-national government banks

Islamic Development Bank

For 1995, the following consolidated balance sheet provides an overview of the financial situation of Islamic Development Bank:

Assets		Liabilities	
Cash & liquid funds	728	Issued & paid-up capital	1,882
Investments	1,231	Reserves	587
Hedging Deposits	182	Special Assistance Account	862
Special/Trust Funds	153	Deposits	167
Murabaha	30	Investment Deposit Scheme	51
Trade and Project Finance	1,322	Other liabilities	176
Other	146	Profit / loss	67
Total assets	3,792	Total liabilities	3,792

Table 14. 1995 Balance sheet of
Islamic Development Bank

Key financial figures on income include:

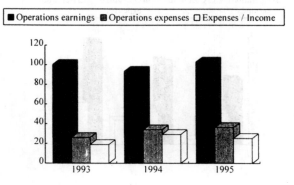

Illustration 18. 1993-1995 Income statements of
Islamic Development Bank

b) Albaraka Investment and Development Company

Albaraka Islamic Investment Bank

For 1995, the following consolidated balance sheet provides an overview of the financial situation of Albaraka Islamic Investment Bank:

Assets $		Liabilities $	
Balances with central banks	13,235,414	Authorised capital	200,000,000
Balances with other banks	8,986,448	Issued & paid-up capital	50,000,000
Islamic financing	117,445,784	Reserves	4,132,054
Investment	13,191,204	Due to central bank	6,665,686
Fixed assets	1,818,809	Deposits	87,275,800
		Other liabilities	5,106,537
Other	2,122,276	Proposed dividends	2,500,000
		Profit / loss	1,119,858
Total assets	156,799,935	Total liabilities	156,799,935

Table 15. 1995 Balance sheet of
Albaraka Islamic Investment Bank

Key financial figures on income (in $ million) include:

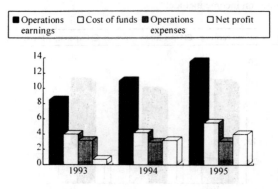

Illustration 19. 1993-1995 Income statements of
Albaraka Islamic Investment Bank

150

c) Arab Banking Corporation

1. Bahrain Islamic Bank

In 1994, authorised capital was BD 23,000,000, of which BD 11,500,000 was issued and paid. Bahrain Islamic Bank's liabilities totalled BD 135,566,000, while assets amounted to BD 149,893,000.

2. ABC International Bank plc

For 1995, the following consolidated balance sheet provides an overview of the financial situation of ABC International Bank plc:

Assets £ 000		Liabilities £ 000	
Cash & liquid funds	119	Capital	150,000
Investments	171,579	Reserves	43,861
Loans	914,399	Deposits	772,086
Debt securities	87,438	Bonds & loan capital	247,622
		Interest and other liabilities	26,819
Other	96,404	Profit / loss	29,551
Total assets	1,269,939	Total liabilities	1,269,939

Table 16. 1995 Balance sheet of ABC International Bank plc

Key financial figures on income include:

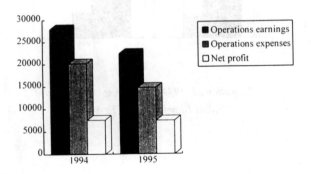

Illustration 20. 1994-1995 Income statements of ABC International Bank plc

151

d) Local Islamic banks

1. Faisal Islamic Bank of Egypt S.A.

For 1995, the following balance sheet provides an overview of the financial situation of Faisal Islamic Bank of Egypt S.A.:

Assets Egyptian £ 000		Liabilities Egyptian £ 000	
Cash & banks	1,223,084.00	Deposits	6,037,596.00
Investments	4,852,981.00		
Premises	31,541.00	Capital	154,962.00
Other	118,868.00	Reserves	33,916.00
Total assets	6,226,474.00	Total liabilities	6,226,474.00

Table 17. 1995 Balance sheet of
Faisal Islamic Bank of Egypt S.A.

Key financial figures on income (in Egyptian £ millions) include:

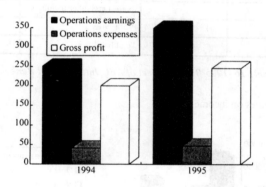

Illustration 21. 1994-1995 Income statements of
Faisal Islamic Bank of Egypt S.A.

2. Faisal Islamic Bank of Kibris Limited

For 1994, the following consolidated balance sheet provides an overview of the financial situation of Faisal Islamic Bank of Kibris Limited:

Assets TL 000,000		Liabilities TL 000,000	
Cash & liquid funds	103,181	Authorised capital	50,000
Investment Certificate		Issued & paid-up capital	10,000
Debit Balances	710,554	Reserves	20,667
Investments	2,315	Deposits	814,037
Tangible Fixed Assets	32,524	Bonds & loan capital	
Other		Other liabilities	3,870
Total assets	848,574	Total liabilities	848,574

Table 18. 1994 Balance sheet of
Faisal Islamic Bank of Kibris Limited

Key financial figures on income include:

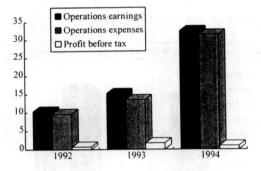

Illustration 22. 1992-1994 Income statements of
Faisal Islamic Bank of Kibris Limited

3.   Malayan Banking Berhad

For 1995, the following consolidated balance sheet provides an overview of the financial situation of Malayan Banking Berhad:

Assets RM 000		Liabilities RM 000	
Cash & liquid funds	8,945,907	Authorised capital	2,000,000
Investments	8,610,045	Issued & paid-up capital	1,143,414
Loans	32,542,946	Reserves	2,743,420
		Deposits	47,549,032
Central Bank deposits	3,170,305	Bonds & loan capital	2,438,850
		Bills payable	4,440,532
Other	6,739,390	Other liabilities	1,449395
		Certificates of deposit	243,950
Total assets	60,008,593	Total liabilities	60,008,593

Table 19. 1995 Balance sheet of
Malayan Banking Berhad

Key financial figures on income (in RM 000) include:

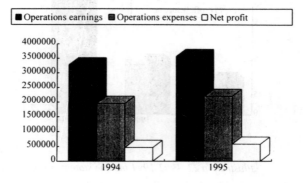

Illustration 23. 1993-1995 Income statements of
Malayan Banking Berhad

4.   Bank Islam Malaysia Berhad

For 1995, the following consolidated balance sheet provides an overview of the financial situation of Bank Islam Malaysia Berhad:

Assets RM 000		Liabilities RM 000	
Cash & liquid funds	56,743	Issued & paid-up capital	133,405
Investments	1,147,961	Reserves	99,807
Loans	1,439,664	Deposits	2,865,963
		Bonds & loan capital	3,768
		Bills payable	26,296
		Other liabilities	95,109
Other	603,955	Subsidiaries	23,975
Total assets	3,248,323	Total liabilities	3,248,323

Table 20. 1995 Balance sheet of
Bank Islam Malaysia Berhad

Key financial figures on income include:

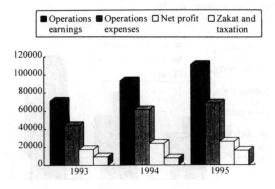

Illustration 24. 1993-1995 Income statements of
Bank Islam Malaysia Berhad

5.   Bank Muamalat

For 1994, the following consolidated balance sheet provides an overview of the financial situation of Bank Muamalat:

Assets Rp.		Liabilities Rp.	
Cash	1,224,773,398	Authorised capital	500,000,000,000
Liquid funds	30,224,180,231	Issued & paid-up capital	94,289,882,000
Investments	2,688,120,000	Reserves	5,512,327,889
Loans	188,844,253,647	Wadiah giro accounts	31,943,994,115
		Other giro accounts	563,006,689
		Mudharabah	100,927,072,232
Other		Other liabilities	7,545,000,770
		Profit / loss	5,286,897,321
Total assets	246,068,181,016	Total liabilities	246,068,181,016

Table 21. 1994 Balance sheet of
Bank Muamalat

Key financial figures on income include:

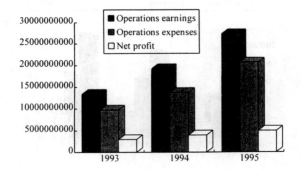

Illustration 25. 1993-1995 Income statements of
Bank Muamalat

156

e) The case of Pakistan

   1.   Muslim Commercial Bank

For 1995, the following consolidated balance sheet provides an overview of the financial situation of Muslim Commercial Bank:

Assets Pak. rupees		Liabilities Pak. rupees	
Cash	14,622,207,578	Authorised capital	2,000,000,000
Liquid funds	1,769,750,918	Issued & paid-up capital	1,517,117,930
Investments	43,951,662,121	Reserves	1,951,196,120
Loans	51,047,969,134	Deposits	99,641,143,853
		Bonds & loan capital	7,049,489,323
		Bills payable	1,967,540,163
Other	37,248,958,525	Other liabilities	36,513,662,946
		Profit / loss	397,941
Total assets	148,640,548,276	Total liabilities	148,640,548,276

Table 22. 1995 Balance sheet of
Muslim Commercial Bank

Key financial figures on income (in Pak. rupees million) include:

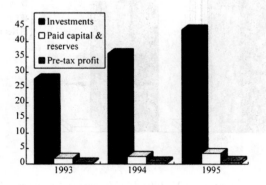

Illustration 26. 1993-1995 Income statements of
Muslim Commercial Bank

2. Agricultural Development Bank of Pakistan

For 1995, the following consolidated balance sheet provides an overview of the financial situation of Agricultural Development Bank of Pakistan:

Assets Pak. rupees		Liabilities Pak. rupees	
Cash & liquid funds	1,726,082,602	Authorised capital	4,000,000,000
Investments	1,499,434,700	Issued & paid-up capital	3,214,323,000
Loans	48,036,086,233	Reserves	3,214,323,000
		Deposits	2,506,267,947
		Bonds & loan capital	48,003,749,456
		Adjustment	172,219,555
Other	10,209,441,465	Other liabilities	237,528,076
		Profit / loss	122,633,966
Total assets	61,471,045,000	Total liabilities	61,471,045,000

Table 23. 1995 Balance sheet of
Agricultural Development Bank of Pakistan

Key financial figures on income (in Pak. rupees million) include:

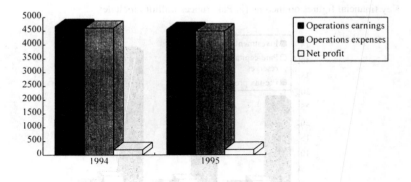

Illustration 27. 1994-1995 Income statements of
Agricultural Development Bank of Pakistan

3. Industrial Development Bank of Pakistan

For 1995, the following consolidated balance sheet provides an overview of the financial situation of Industrial Development Bank of Pakistan:

Assets Pak. rupees		Liabilities Pak. rupees	
Cash & liquid funds	800,978,000	Authorised, issued & paid-up capital	157,000,000
Investments	1,975,678,000	Reserves	745,880,000
Loans	13,517,401,000	Deposits	7,704,314,000
		Bonds & loan capital	9,487,763,000
		Bills payable	2,051,517,000
		Liabilities Bangladesh	779,554,000
Other	4,640,943,000	Other	8,972,000
Total assets	20,935,000,000	Total liabilities	20,935,000,000

Table 24. 1995 Balance sheet of
Industrial Development Bank of Pakistan

Key financial figures on income (in Pak. rupees million) include:

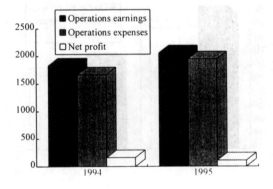

Illustration 28. 1993-1995 Income statements of
Industrial Development Bank of Pakistan

159

4. Saudi-Pak Industrial & Agricultural Investment Company (PVT) Ltd

For 1995, the following consolidated balance sheet provides an overview of the financial situation of Saudi-Pak Industrial & Agricultural Investment Company (PVT) Ltd:

Assets Pak. rupees		Liabilities Pak. rupees	
Cash & liquid funds	435,878,332	Authorised, issued & paid-up capital	1,756,620,000
Investments	1,529,637,617	Reserves	939,254,941
Term finances	1,148,638,226	Deferred liability	2,665,333
Short term finances	5,056,750,550	Deferred income	21,529,928
		Short term finances	7,207,254,359
Other	2,067,762,731	Other liabilities	311,342,895
Total assets	10,238,667,456	Total liabilities	10,238,667,456

Table 25. 1995 Balance sheet of
Saudi-Pak Industrial & Agricultural Investment Company (PVT) Ltd

Key financial figures on income (in Pak. rupees million) include:

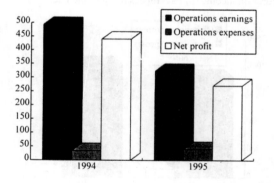

Illustration 29. 1994-1995 Income statements of
Saudi-Pak Industrial & Agricultural Investment Company (PVT) Ltd

5. First Women Bank Limited

For 1995, the following consolidated balance sheet provides an overview of the financial situation of First Women Bank Limited:

Assets Pak. rupees		Liabilities Pak. rupees	
Cash	377,430,680	Issued & paid-up capital	200,000,000
Liquid funds	885,599,343	Reserves	21,264,915
Investments	1,065,907,430	Deposits	2,392,220,567
Loans	340,542,135	Bonds & loan capital	126,350,998
Other	300,330,134	Other liabilities	166,898,668
		Profit / loss	63,074,574
Total assets	2,969,809,722	Total liabilities	2,969,809,722

Table 26. 1995 Balance sheet of
First Women Bank Limited

Key financial figures on income (in Pak. rupees million) include:

Illustration 30. 1994-1995 Income statements of
First Women Bank Limited

3. Co-operative banking in Europe

a) Banks of ethical origin

1. DG Bank

For 1995, the following figures (DM 000,000) provides an overview of the financial situation of DG Bank:

	30/12/1994	30/06/1995
Balance	143,183	141,821
Volume of business	151,021	149,063
Volume of credits	77,221	76,031
Funds under management	124,792	123,419
Attested securities	18,727	18,568
Own resources	4,147	4,319

Table 27. 1994-1995 Financial overview of DG Bank

Key financial figures on income include:

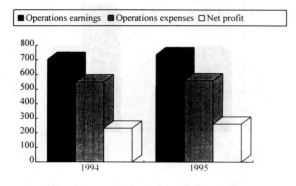

Illustration 31. 1994-1995 Income statements of DG Bank

2. Berliner Volksbank eG

For 1995, the following consolidated balance sheet provides an overview of the financial situation of Berliner Volksbank eG:

Assets DM		Liabilities DM	
Cash & banks	4,359,115,765.61	Deposits	12,158,046,101.61
Investments	1,014,937,272.31	Other liabilities	133,122,556.47
Loans & Discounts	6,828,748,802.93	Capital	336,380,929.94
Premises	359,821,431.00	Reserves	621,166,938.29
Other	709,793,254.46	Profit / loss	23,700,000.00
Total assets	13,272,416,526.31	Total liabilities	13,272,416,526.31

Table 28. 1995 Balance sheet of
Berliner Volksbank eG

Key financial figures on income (in DM 000) include:

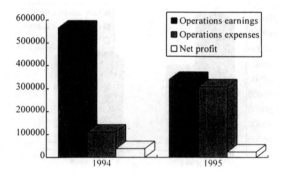

Illustration 32. 1994-1995 Income statements of
Berliner Volksbank eG

In the client base, no distinction is made on the basis of religion.

3.   Frankfurter Volksbank eG

For 1995, the following consolidated balance sheet provides an overview of the financial
situation of Frankfurter Volksbank eG:

Assets DM		Liabilities DM	
Cash & banks	745,213,337.43	Deposits	4,408,948,451.30
Investments	930,592,782.05	Other liabilities	243,569,567.36
Loans	3,009,144,390.98	Capital	135,739,081.53
Premises	77,309,852.87	Reserves	173,088,942.98
Other	208,417,606.30	Profit / loss	9,331,926.46
Total assets	4,970,677,969.63	Total liabilities	4,970,677,969.63

Table 29. 1995 Balance sheet of
Frankfurter Volksbank eG

Key financial figures on income include:

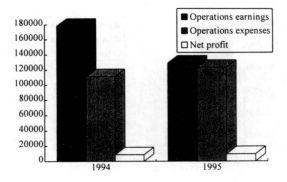

Illustration 33. 1994-1995 Income statements of
Frankfurter Volksbank eG

With respect to the client base, no distinction is made on the basis of religion and no
record is kept of religious affiliations.

4. Südwestbank AG

For 1995, the following consolidated balance sheet provides an overview of the financial situation of Südwestbank AG:

Assets DM		Liabilities DM	
Cash & banks	762,952,901.76	Deposits	4,665,761,425.40
Investments	521,676,063.30	Other liabilities	185,699,084.08
Loans & Discounts	3,703,877,684.98	Capital	209,054,634.50
Premises	88,429,800.00	Reserves	91,095,822.77
Other	82,234,516.71	Profit / loss	7,560,000.00
Total assets	5,159,170,966.75	Total liabilities	5,159,170,966.75

Table 30. 1995 Balance sheet of
Südwestbank AG

Key financial figures on income (in DM 000) include:

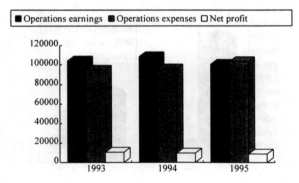

Illustration 34. 1993-1995 Income statements of
Südwestbank AG

165

5. Deutsche Apotheker- u. Ärztebank eG

For 1995, the following consolidated balance sheet provides an overview of the financial situation of Deutsche Apotheker- u. Ärztebank eG:

Assets DM		Liabilities DM	
Cash & banks	3,943,255,032.87	Deposits	20,398,920,283.55
Investments	2,812,886,114.57	Other liabilities	432,378,778.88
Loans & Discounts	15,006,725,595.09	Capital	697,416,715.92
Premises	257,374,162.92	Reserves	615,033,129.94
Other	194,408,383.51	Profit / loss	70,900,380.67
Total assets	22,214,649,288.96	Total liabilities	22,214,649,288.96

Table 31. 1995 Balance sheet of
Deutsche Apotheker- u. Ärztebank eG

Key financial figures on income (in DM 000) include:

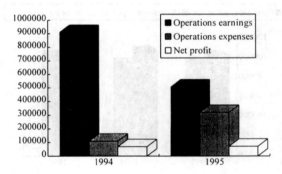

Illustration 35. 1992-1995 Income statements of
Deutsche Apotheker- u. Ärztebank eG

In the client base, no distinction is made on the basis of religion and no record is kept of religious affiliations.

b) Religion guided banks

1. Bank für Kirche und Diakonie eG

For 1995, the following consolidated balance sheet provides an overview of the financial situation of Bank für Kirche und Diakonie eG:

Assets DM		Liabilities DM	
Cash & banks	1,295,260,942.83	Deposits	3,079,571,606.17
Investments	1,006,282,294.79	Other liabilities	5,750,036.16
Loans & Discounts	895,772,763.53	Capital	31,478,450.00
Premises	7,405,731.25	Reserves	90,651,891.52
Other	5,333,597.47	Profit / loss	2,603,346.02
Total assets	3,210,055,329.87	Total liabilities	3,210,055,329.87

Table 32. 1995 Balance sheet of
Bank für Kirche und Diakonie eG

Key financial figures on income (in DM 000) include:

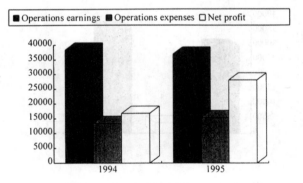

Illustration 36. 1993-1995 Income statements of
Bank für Kirche und Diakonie eG

2. Evangelische Darlehnsgenossenschaft eG

For 1995, the following consolidated balance sheet provides an overview of the financial situation of the Evangelische Darlehnsgenossenschaft eG:

Assets DM		Liabilities DM	
Cash & banks	1,337,028,810.29	Deposits	5,704,164,812.87
Investments	3,360,702,487.56	Other liabilities	2,823,920.36
Loans & Discounts	1,191,091,644.94	Capital	123,313,700.00
Premises	13,763,087.95	Reserves	74,855,522.20
Other	6,538,709.45	Profit / loss	3,966,784.76
Total assets	5,909,124,740.19	Total liabilities	5,909,124,740.19

Table 33. 1995 Balance sheet of
Evangelische Darlehnsgenossenschaft eG

Key financial figures on income include:

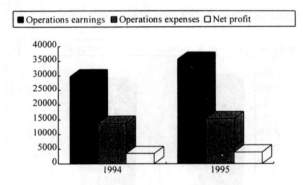

Illustration 37. 1994-1995 Income statements of
Evangelische Darlehnsgenossenschaft eG

c) Non-religious ethical banks

1. Crédit Coopératif

The bank's solidarity funds are highly successful in the market in terms of subscription and of capital performance. They have also created an excellent visibility of Crédit Coopératif in the media which means that the bank performed very well.

2.   The Co-operative Bank

For 1995, the following consolidated balance sheet provides an overview of the financial situation of The Co-operative Bank:

Assets £ 000		Liabilities £ 000	
Cash & banks	994,511.00	Deposits	3,406,510.00
Investments	713,720.00	Other liabilities	326,646.00
Loans & Discounts	2,090,178.00	Capital	90,000.00
Premises	52,367.00	Reserves	26,094.00
Other	72,796.00	Profit / loss	74,322.00
Total assets	3,923,572.00	Total liabilities	3,923,572.00

Table 34. 1995 Balance sheet of
The Co-operative Bank

Key financial figures on income (in £ 000) include:

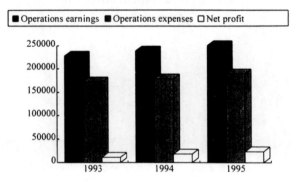

Illustration 38. 1993-1995 Income statements of
The Co-operative Bank

3.   National Federation of Credit Unions

In 1995, the National Federation of Credit Unions totalled £ 27,505,000, while liabilities amounted to £ 21,848,000.

4. Co-operative banking in the Muslim World

Grameen Bank

For 1995, the following figures provide an overview of the financial situation of Grameen Bank:

	Taka	$ 000,000
Cumulative amount disbursed	59,592.91	1,603.70
Amount disbursed Nov 94 - Nov 95	14,837.91	380.5
Cumulative amount of housing loans disbursed	5,368.97	144.18
Cumulative amount of housing loans disbursed Nov 94 - Nov 95	842.18	21.59
Cumulative amount of savings in group fund	4,037.48	108.78
Balance of total savings	651.69	16.71

Table 35. 1995 Financial overview of
Grameen Bank

Thesis summary

The University of Aston in Birmingham: Impact of religion on business ethics in Europe and the Muslim World - Islamic versus Christian tradition. Ingmar Wienen, Master of Science by Research in Business Management, May 1997.

The **concern** of the research project is to assess the extent to which religion influences standards and behaviour in business and whether it is only exerted in business modes which refer explicitly to religion or in other practices as well. The objective is to develop a better understanding of cross-cultural business with a view to finding ways of improving the interaction by referring to common ethical standards. The banking sector is taken as an illustrative example. Within this sector, Islamic banking is compared to co-operative banking in both Europe and the Muslim World. While Christianity is the dominant religion in Europe, Islam is the driving force in the Muslim World.

In **existing work**, the research problem has already been identified, but not solved in a satisfactory manner, because a more interdisciplinary approach is missing. There are, however, intercultural studies, studies on religions and studies on business ethics.

In a **theoretical study**, the relevant elements of the project, i.e. the two sample environments, the two sample religions and their respective ethical systems, and the two modes of operations were to be analysed. Thus, the aspects of the business that can be observed and related to the supposed influence, were established. It was found out that they are particular in the business they accept, i.e. in the kind of products they offer, and in their organisation. The key elements of Islamic banking are the *Islamic financial instruments*. On the other hand, it is the *organisation* which is key to co-operative banking.

It was then planned to investigate in the current practices of Islamic banking in Europe and the Muslim World, and similarly in the practice of co-operative banking in both environments. In the **empirical investigation** it was found out that Islamic banks offer conventional banking products as well as specifically Islamic ones. These banks could therefore be described as conventional banks with some modifications in the product range according to religious, i.e. Islamic, interdictions. Co-operative banks operate in a way that allows mutual help among the poor. Religion, i.e. Christian Faith in Europe and Islam in the Muslim World, provides the objective of these banks 'to help the poor'.

As a **result** it can be said that there is an influence of religion, i.e. of Christian Faith and Islam, on business ethics, expressed in different modes of operation in the banking sector. This influence is varying. Islamic banking is an ethical system which can be shared fundamentally by Muslims only because it is built on Muslim faith. Co-operative banking can be described as a system in which Christians and Muslims share the same ethical principles in that they share the objective to care for their neighbour and to overcome poverty. By referring to this common ethical standard, Muslims and Christians have an opportunity to work together to foster development and to overcome poverty.

Key words: Islamic banking, Co-operative banking, Ethical banking, Culture, Self-help.

Werner Kaltefleiter / Ulrike Schumacher (eds.)

The Rise of a Multipolar World

Papers presented at the Summer Course 1997 on International Security

Frankfurt/M., Berlin, Bern, New York, Paris, Wien, 1998. 214 pp., 1 fig., 9 tab.
Conflicts, Options, Strategies in a Threatened World.
Edited by Werner Kaltefleiter and Ulrike Schumacher. Vol. 2
ISBN 3-631-33286-6 · pb. DM 65.–*
US-ISBN 0-8204-3592-9

The international system which was characterized by its bipolar structure until the end of the systemic conflict undergoes a process of change. New regional power centres seem to emerge in various parts of the world. Those centres have begun to position themselves in different roles in their regions. China seems to be on its way towards a position as hegemon in the Asia-Pacific region. India is trying to determine its foreign policy under new auspices after the end of the concept of non-aligned states. Brazil seems to be using its geostrategic position to dominate the South American continent. Those are some examples of the change in the international system from bipolarity to multipolarity. In order to restructure the international community, several approaches can be discussed. Will the United States of America be the world's only superpower? Or, will the United Nations be able to provide collective security? The lectures presented at the Summer Course on International Security 1997 attempt to at least partially answer these questions.

Contents: After the end of the systemic conflict regional powers have gained a new role in the international system: among these are India, China, Brazil, and Germany · Methods of conflict resolution by international institutions and democratic control are discussed

Frankfurt/M · Berlin · Bern · New York · Paris · Wien
Distribution: Verlag Peter Lang AG
Jupiterstr. 15, CH-3000 Bern 15
Fax (004131) 9402131
*incl. value added tax
Prices are subject to change without notice.

Sidebar (vertical text): Peter Lang · Europäischer Verlag der Wissenschaften